W9-AVN-944

78 THINGS THEY DIDN'T TEACH YOU IN SCHOOL

But You *Do* Need To Know

EMILY FALK

rabbit's
foot
press™

A division of SPS Studios
Boulder, Colorado

Library of Congress Catalog Card Number: 2004026020
ISBN: 1-58786-016-3

Certain trademarks are used under license.

Printed in the United States of America.
First Printing: 2004

 This book is printed on recycled paper.

This book is printed on fine quality, laid embossed, 80 lb. paper. This paper has been specially produced to be acid free (neutral pH) and contains no groundwood or unbleached pulp. It conforms with all the requirements of the American National Standards Institute, Inc., so as to ensure that this book will last and be enjoyed by future generations.

Library of Congress Cataloging-in-Publication Data

Falk, Emily, 1981-
   78 things they didn't teach you in school : but you do need to know / Emily Falk.
     p. cm.
   ISBN 1-58786-016-3 (trade pbk. : alk. paper) 1. Life skills—Handbooks, manuals, etc. 2. Young adults—Life skills guides. I. Title: Seventy eight things they didn't teach you in school. II. Title.

   HQ2037.F35 2004
   646.7—dc22

2004026020
CIP

Blue Mountain Arts, Inc.

P.O. Box 4549, Boulder, Colorado 80306

Introduction

Although you have learned many useful things in school such as how to add and subtract, how to share, how not to get caught with your hand in the cookie jar, and how to hit a baseball, there are many things you may have missed. Depending on how far you went, you may be able to define terms such as "didactic," "epistemology," and "predilection." That's great, but many graduates still can't pick out fruit in a supermarket.

78 Things They Didn't Teach You in School is for everyone, not just students. Want tips for how to maintain a relationship with your family once you move out of the house? Flip to page 100. Don't know how to change a tire? Go to page 95. You'll learn how to be a better traveler, how to dress for job interviews, and tons of other fun and useful information — including how to pick out fruit in the supermarket.

There are often several ways of doing something right. This guide will give you short cuts and tricks to help you get things done more easily and quickly and ideas to develop on your own.

The *Vocabulary They Didn't Teach You* boxes will help you sound like you know what you're talking about and impress your friends. Short, clear explanations will give you the knowledge you need to get each job done. After reading this book, you will also be better equipped to find extra information on your own. So roll up your sleeves and get ready to discover all the things they didn't teach you in school, but you *do* need to know.

Taking Care of
Your Body

EAT WELL
•• Buying Groceries Without Going Broke ••

✓ **Get a membership card** at the stores you use most to receive automatic savings.

✓ **Clip coupons.** The Sunday paper is full of bargains. Look for stores that give double coupons.

✓ **Buy non-perishable foods in bulk** (cereal, flour, rice, pasta, detergent, etc.). Buy onions and potatoes in large bags and store them in a cool, dry place. There are stores that specialize in family-sized packages of things like cereal and toilet paper — become a member and go once a month to stock up on necessities. If you have the space, freeze grains to keep them fresh.

✓ **Find a few friends** and split groceries. Taking turns shopping will save you time, and buying in bulk means paying less. You could even take turns cooking — another time saver.

✓ **Generic products** are often comparable to their brand-name equivalents, but people overlook this money-saving option because they think brand name equals quality. Often, however, both brand-name and generic products are made using exactly the same techniques in exactly the same factories. You may not be able to tell the difference, especially with items that are simple to produce (milk, eggs, flour, etc.) and with things that you don't taste (pills, cleaning products). However, there are exceptions. I generally prefer brand-name ice cream, so while I save on other food, I splurge on the desserts I like. I also go for pricier mayonnaise and ketchup.

✔ **Compare unit prices.** Sometimes items cost the same amount per package, but one contains half as much product. Next to the price tag, find the price per pound or per volume. This is a better number for comparing value than the price per package.

✔ **Cut down on prepared foods.** I admit that it's nice to come home, open a can of soup, microwave it, and be done with preparations. However, a cheaper, healthier, and tastier option is to buy fresh ingredients, make a big batch of soup, and then freeze most of it for later. This will work for many foods that are expensive, prepared, and contain lots of nasty chemical preservatives, fats, and sugars, but are simple and cheap to make yourself. When freezing for later, divide the food into portion sizes so you don't have to defrost the whole batch.

✔ **Check your receipt.** Automated scanners and humans make mistakes. Make sure you weren't overcharged; this happens more often than you might imagine. If you were overcharged, speak to a manager who might even give you the item for free.

✔ **Don't shop when you're hungry.** Going to the supermarket on a full stomach will help you avoid impulse buys, which will not only add to your bill, but also tend to be less nutritious.

✔ **Buy meat on sale and freeze it.** Most meats keep for up to six months in the freezer, so buy when it's cheap. This goes for other food that also freezes well.

•• Picking Out Fruits and Veggies ••

I have a friend who sometimes describes people who are pushovers as "ripe." He chose this word because certain fruits "yield under gentle pressure" when they are ripe and ready to be eaten. Fruits in this category include peaches, pears, and plums.

Buy produce right before it's ripe, if you want it to last a few days. Choose firm contenders that require slightly more than gentle pressure to give in under your thumb.

> **Vocabulary they didn't teach you:** a *drupe* is a fruit with one large, hard seed. Peaches, plums, and almonds are drupes.

For fruits that should be crispy (such as apples), opt for those that do not give in under the pressure of your thumb. You don't want to push so hard as to do damage — a good rule is that if it would hurt you to be pinched with as much pressure as you're applying to the skin of the fruit, it probably hurts the fruit, too.

Smelling is another good way to choose, especially for melons and pineapples. A good melon or pineapple smells sweet. Another way to choose a pineapple is by plucking one of the leaves from the top — if it comes out easily, the fruit is ripe. An under-ripe melon has no smell, while an overripe melon may be slightly sour or sharp. To choose the perfect honeydew melon, shake it. If you hear seeds rattle inside, it is ripe. If not, choose another. In general, choose produce that smells fresh. A large part of our sense of taste comes from smells associated with food. That is why your parents told you to hold your nose when they asked you to eat food you didn't like or to swallow yucky-tasting medicine as a small child. Food that smells good will taste good, too.

•• Organic Food ••

Organic food is grown without chemicals. This means that farmers need to come up with other ways to protect their crops from disease and pests. The extra work involved often makes organic food more expensive at the supermarket, so you may want to buy a mix of organic and non-organic, depending on your budget and what kinds of things you're buying. It's often healthier to buy organic leafy greens like lettuce and spinach since pesticides build up in the crevices and folds of the leaves. It's less important to buy organic food that you peel (oranges, lemons) since you'll discard the outer layer. Even root vegetables, like carrots, can absorb pesticides sprayed on the leaves of the plant, but by cutting off the top inch, you can avoid ingesting most of the chemicals.

When buying vegetables, choose a variety of colors (carrots, spinach, and potatoes, for example) to balance your nutritional needs. Darker leafy greens have more nutritional value than lighter ones. Don't opt for iceberg lettuce if you want vitamins. Avoid veggies with soft, mushy spots, although some discolorations can be peeled off.

When picking out any produce, do not be fooled by colors. Although visual inspection is an important way to weed out rotten or otherwise undesirable products, your eyes may deceive you. Don't pick the shiniest, reddest apples simply for their aesthetic appeal; color and luster can be added with dye and wax. You may notice that organic produce lacks the bright colors and shine of its non-organic counterpart, but it tastes just as good and sometimes better.

•• Don't Forget to Check Dates ••

Always check the expiration dates on certain items. If the milk you reach for has a date that is fast approaching, reach to the back of the row. Since most supermarkets restock from the back, that is where the freshest stuff usually is. You should also check expiration dates for yogurt, cottage cheese, eggs, juice, meat, and any other dairy or egg-based product. It's always good to check!

•• Getting Your Groceries Home ••

✔ When you go shopping, consider your transportation. If you are walking, wait until next time to buy heavy liquids or laundry detergent.

✔ Trade turns shopping with friends. You help them carry their groceries once a week and in exchange they do the same for you. That way, you'll get as much as you would in two trips, but you'll also have company. If you just moved and don't have friends yet, turn to page 104.

✔ Plan ahead. Think about how much time you will have for shopping, what you really need, and what can wait until you are able to do a big shopping trip (i.e., when you can borrow a friend's car).

✔ In cities, many stores offer delivery service — you buy what you want, and for a fee, they deliver it to your home.

•• Cooking for Yourself Without Getting Poisoned ••

Tips for working in the kitchen:
✓Always wash your hands before cooking or eating.
✓Clean up as you go along. You'll be glad you did at the end.
✓Keep your knives sharp and never wash them in a dishwasher.

Experiment. Think about what you'd like to eat, and then think about what flavors could be added to make it better. Once you have chosen your ingredients, there are lots of ways to prepare them. For example, one of the simplest dishes is pasta, but it can be combined with a wide variety of sauces (also simple to make) to create many different flavors.

Did you know... you can freeze cooked pasta? Just remember to cook it for a little less time initially, as you will have to reheat it when you want to eat it.

Try pasta with red sauce: sauté raw tomatoes and onions for about ten minutes in olive oil, add salt and pepper, and serve over pasta. Or with garlic and oil: get the oil hot, then take it off the heat. Sauté garlic in the heated olive oil until it gets soft, add salt, and serve over pasta. Don't try to salvage burned garlic — it will only make your food bitter. Or try pasta with lentils: open one can of precooked lentils, add chopped basil, and serve over pasta with a dollop of sour cream. For a cheaper and only slightly more difficult option, buy dried lentils, boil four cups of water, dump in half a cup of lentils (for one person), cook them for an hour with a bay leaf, drain, and add some salt. Continue as above.

> *"Cook with attitude. When cooking sauce, be saucy."*
> — Aaron, 21, unemployed.

This formula works in many situations. Start with simple ingredients, then think about what different things you can add to make the dish interesting. For example, there are about a million ways to prepare potatoes — fried, mashed, sautéed with herbs, shredded and patted into pancakes, baked, etc. Use your imagination.

To open a stubborn jar:
My friend Allie's grandma uses a rubber band. Placing it around the lid will give you the extra traction you need to get the jar open. The rubber band method is great for nail polish bottles, too.

I like to run the jar under hot water, which usually loosens the lid enough to get it off. Sometimes, in a pinch, I also tap the lid on the floor.

If you're lazy, spring for a "jar opener." This can be purchased at any home store and makes the job a piece of cake.

•• Cooking Options ••

Here are some basic methods you may not have tried. Go ahead — experiment! It's easier than you think.

> *"Don't be afraid of the kitchen. If you just start, it gets a lot easier."*
>
> — Sharon, 19, activist

Frying. You will need a pan and oil, or butter. Start with dry ingredients (i.e., if you want to fry chicken, press it between paper towels first to absorb the extra liquid). Turn often or else your food will burn. Try coating your ingredients in egg and rolling them in breadcrumbs before frying. This is a good way to make chicken nuggets.

Sautéing. You will also need a pan and oil, butter, or cooking spray for sautéing, but unlike frying, it involves a much smaller amount. You are using high heat to cook small pieces of food very quickly. Use high to medium heat and stir often.

Marinating. Bathe your ingredients in a sauce before cooking them, allowing them to soak up the taste of the sauce. This is an easy way to make simple ingredients taste fancy. Vinegar, soy sauce, oil, and herbs are some of my favorite ingredients for a marinade. When using vinegar or soy sauce for a marinade, balance the acidity with something lighter and sweeter such as a touch of honey or even apricot jam. Scallions and ginger are a nice addition, as are sesame seeds, which are high in calcium.

For meat, try teriyaki or Worcestershire sauce and garlic.

Put your marinade in a pan or baggie, then add the meat. Place everything in the fridge for about an hour, turning the ingredients every once in a while, then fry or bake.

Steaming. This is exactly what it sounds like — cooking ingredients with steam. This is a quick, easy, and healthy way to cook veggies. You will need a pot and a metal colander. Put about an inch of water in the bottom of the pot and put your ingredients (usually vegetables) in the colander. Place the colander in the pot so that the veggies hover over the water and aren't immersed. Turn on the heat. When the water at the bottom starts to boil, the steam cooks your food. This leaves vegetables more tender and flavorful than boiling. Your **microwave** can also steam veggies.

> **Douglas's finger trick for perfect rice:**
> To make the perfect bowl of rice for one or two people, fill an average bowl halfway with dry rice and cover it with water until the water level is about an inch above the rice level (which you can measure by sticking your finger above the rice and filling water to the first joint). Put it in a pot, cover it, and cook it until it boils, then leave it on very low heat for about ten minutes. Another way to measure is to use about one cup of water for every cup of rice.

Microwaving. This method can be applied to fine cuisine as well as to TV dinners. For example, to cook a bell pepper in a flash, wash it, cut out the seeds, wrap it in plastic wrap, and microwave it for a little less than a minute, depending on your machine's power — a little longer will get you pimento. Asparagus, broccoli, carrots, potatoes, turnips, zucchini, and green beans all cook well in the microwave. As I mentioned earlier, you can also steam vegetables in a microwave. Add a small amount of water to the bottom of a microwaveable bowl. Place veggies in the bowl, cover with another upside-down bowl or plastic wrap, and zap it. Be careful when you remove the cover because it's easy to burn yourself with the steam.

Grilling. Like frying, you can grill almost anything. Fire up your grill so it gets nice and hot. Marinate your ingredients either in sauce or olive oil. Place them directly on the grill and cover. Grilling gives food a smoky, charred taste that goes well with barbecue sauce. Grilling is also healthier than most methods of cooking because it allows fat to drip into the fire and out of your diet. Avoid charring when using charcoal since the black part is carcinogenic.

Baking. Any time you put something in the oven, you are baking. If you don't want the top to brown (or burn), cover it with aluminum foil. If you want something to cook all the way through, cook it on low heat for a long time. If you want the outside to be crispy, cook it on high for less time. Some baked foods, such as chicken, look and taste better if they are browned in a pan on top of the stove before being baked.

Broiling. Broiling involves cooking ingredients under high heat. You will need a broiler (the really hot part of an oven that's located below the main compartment), and a heavy pan. This technique is usually used for meat and works best with thin cuts, as thicker cuts tend to burn before the inside is cooked. Place your meat on a rack over a pan and slide it under the broiler. Wait a few minutes, check to see if it's crispy, and then turn it over. Broiling is also great for making garlic bread. Spread butter or olive oil on a loaf, add crushed garlic, cover, and cook it under the broiler until crisp. Be sure to watch it because the whole process could take only a minute or two.

Braising. For thicker cuts of meat, try braising, which involves frying the meat until brown, then adding liquid (wine or stock), and cooking it on lower heat until the meat is tender. This will take a long time. You can try braising vegetables for a different, sweeter effect. Braised celery or parsnips are delicious. **Roasting** is braising without the liquid. Roasted veggies are impressive at parties and are so simple to prepare — olive oil, salt, and pepper are all it takes.

Blending/Pureeing. With a blender or food processor, you can make smoothies (add any combination of fruit, juice, milk, protein powder, ice cream, etc., for a delicious treat), or a great soup base. For the latter, boil or sauté veggies until they are soft and then blend them to make a thick base for a soup. Add water for a traditional stock or milk for a creamy one.

SLEEP WELL
•• How to Fall Asleep More Easily ••

"I thought coffee was enough to keep me awake during the day, but then I tried actually getting enough sleep at night. What a difference! I feel so much better now, and I'm much more efficient."

— Gail, 25, consultant

Here are a few quick tips to improve the sleep you can get in the time you have:

✔ Keep reading this book (or another classic). Reading in general makes many people sleepy.

✔ Keep to a regular schedule. This helps your body remember bedtime, even when your mind doesn't.

✔ Stress prevents many people from sleeping. To combat stress, exercise. You don't need to run marathons; you just need to be active. Exercising will give you more energy during the day, but will let you get better sleep at night. Other stress busters include talking to friends, laughing, being outside, taking deep breaths, and drinking water. Many people hold their breath without even realizing it when they are stressed. Making a conscious effort to breathe from the diaphragm is invaluable.

✔ Watch your diet. Avoid caffeine in the evening. Caffeine isn't just in coffee. Most dark sodas have caffeine, too, so if you're sensitive to it, beware. Some people think that citrus fruits are stimulants as well. Artificial colors and flavors, alcohol, and Monosodium Glutamate (MSG) can also interfere with sleep.

✔ Eat enough at dinner so that your stomach isn't growling before bed, but try to avoid heavy meals right before you hit the hay — especially proteins since they are harder to digest.

✔ Avoid drinking alcohol during the week — even though it's a sedative, the sleep you get under the influence is less restful.

✔ People who use their beds only for sleeping have an easier time falling asleep at night, so set rules for yourself — avoid bringing your work with you to bed, both mentally and physically. Try to avoid thinking about deadlines or stressful topics while in your resting space.

✔ You can also try a relaxation exercise: tighten and relax every part of your body starting with your toes, and work your way up. Focus on your breathing — stomach out on the inhale and in on the exhale makes for a deep, diaphragmatic breath rather than a shallow, chest one.

✔ Limit naps to twenty minutes, and, if possible, separate them from your work time and space. One- or two-hour naps may actually make you feel more tired.

EXERCISE
•• Finding the Time ••

Sure, we all know that it would be beneficial to join a gym or to get up every morning and go for a jog. If you're like I am, though, it might be hard to get motivated to exercise. Stop making excuses. When it comes to exercise, experts disagree about what constitutes "enough," but, in general, you will feel better and sleep better if you do *something*.

The hardest part is getting started, so do it with a friend. You'll help motivate each other and after the first few outings, you'll be good to go on your own. Try to be active at least twenty minutes a day. It can be spread out over two ten-minute walks, if that fits your schedule better.

On days when you have more time, try to do more. Also try to be more active on days when you are stressed. Shaking your booty will help dissipate tension. Make time for yourself. If you get an hour for lunch, eat during the first twenty minutes then go for a walk. Getting outside will give you fresh air, and a walk will add to your exercise quotient.

> **Get moving!** Go dancing on the weekend or have friends over and rent a Latin dance video. Let loose and be silly learning to salsa or cha-cha. Even if you aren't ready to take on Enrique Iglesias, you'll get your heart pumping. Take pictures: laughter is also good for you.

If you're injured or don't have a lot of time to move around and get your heart pumping, stretch. Flexibility is almost as important as cardiovascular strength. Try to move around a little bit at your desk — crimp, point, and flex your toes, use a stress ball, or lift one leg, then the other. Studies have actually shown that when people are deprived of physical activity, those who fidget more stay slimmer!

Shoe clue: Keep a pair of comfortable shoes handy at the office. Put them on at lunch and go for a quick walk. This will not only help your physical health, but will also increase your concentration and productivity.

Still, if none of this appeals to you, don't despair. You can fit more calorie busting into a normal day than you'd think. Scrubbing yourself in the shower works arm muscles. So does moving boxes. Rearrange your room. Moving furniture is great exercise, but watch your back. Biking to work will save time waiting for the bus, and will also get your cardiovascular system working. Being late can be good for you; walking quickly boosts your heart rate and gets your endorphins pumping.

Vocabulary they didn't teach you: *Endorphins* are chemicals that are released during exercise, triggering the feel-good center in your brain. Endorphins actually make you less sensitive to both physical and emotional pain!

•• Exercising the Inexpensive Way ••

If you want to exercise without spending a lot, you might try dangling a little piece of cake from a stick in front of your face just out of reach, then chase it. Or, if you'd feel silly doing that, use your own body weight to your advantage — it's free to do sit-ups, crunches, pushups, squats, and pull-ups.

To save money, you can also make your own weights. If you're the competitive type, have a contest with your friends or coworkers to see who can do the most arm curls with a liter of water (which weighs about 2.2 pounds). If one liter is too light, move up to a gallon (which weighs about 8.3 pounds). If you're not the competitive type, you can still use these common items to avoid buying expensive weights.

> "I never used to work out at all — I just didn't have time. Then my office was moved from the ground floor to the third. I started taking the stairs because the elevator in our building is ridiculously slow, and I've actually noticed that I feel a lot better."
> — Annie, sales executive, 26

Take the stairs at work. If you work on the tenth floor, get off the elevator on the seventh and walk the rest of the way. Get off your local public transportation one or two stops before you normally would or park your car farther away than usual and walk quickly to work.

If you want to get serious with your workouts, many towns organize intramural leagues. Joining a team is not only a good way

25

to work out, it's also a good way to meet people. Some cities also offer free training in preparation for marathons and triathlons. They recoup the money spent to get you in shape with money from sponsors of the event.

HEALTH CARE
•• Getting Insured ••

Health insurance is important because it helps make your medical visits affordable, but more importantly, it protects you if you ever need a big operation or emergency care. When these types of incidents occur, hospital visits can be *extremely* costly and are really only possible if you're insured. Once you reach a certain age, usually in your early twenties, you become ineligible for coverage under your parents' health insurance, assuming you were lucky enough to be covered in the first place. Whether you have just reached this point, are graduating from college and losing the benefits of your student plan, or are looking to get coverage for the first time, you should first ask yourself some basic questions:

Am I already eligible for coverage?
Check with your parents to see if they have a health plan, and if so, whether you can be added for a reasonable fee. Buying your own independent plan may be extremely expensive.

Depending on your income level and age, you may also be eligible for government plans such as Medicaid or Medicare. Look online or check with your local legal agency or hospital to obtain information about government-subsidized health plans in your state. Many states offer this type of plan for children under eighteen.

How much money can I reasonably put aside each month for health insurance?

Remember that the more money you put into your health plan, the less you will pay for individual visits, prescriptions, etc. Typically, cheaper plans will cover emergency care, but will give you less choice about which doctors you are allowed to see and will require a larger co-pay. In general, it is best to pay a little more each month if you can get prescription coverage, dental coverage, and optical coverage, which are all add-ons, or if you can get a lower co-pay. This will not only reduce your costs, but will also make you more likely to seek out the care you need in the first place.

> **Vocabulary they didn't teach you:** The *co-pay* is the amount of money that you pay out of pocket (at a doctor's office or for prescriptions) while insurance covers the rest. For example, if the bill for a checkup is $100, your insurance might ask you to pay the first $20, and they will cover the rest.

Am I looking for short-term or long-term coverage ?

If you will soon have a health plan from your employer, consider either not leaving the house to avoid injury or getting temporary insurance. This type of coverage can be purchased based on the number of days until you have your new plan. It probably won't cover pre-existing conditions and will be too expensive to use as a long-term option. Shop around online, talk to friends and family about their plans, or use an insurance broker to help you find an insurance agent.

What do I need to know when choosing a health plan?

Make sure you know exactly what the policy does and doesn't cover. A section usually titled "exclusions" will tell you what the plan doesn't cover. Find out if the policy has a prescription plan (it should). If so, make sure that you can use the local pharmacy — many plans restrict the locations where you can buy drugs. Also find out if over-the-counter medication is covered.

Do I plan to travel outside of my home state or outside of the country in the near future?

If you plan to be away from the area normally covered by your basic policy, you can purchase travel insurance (similar to temporary insurance) to cover you while you are out of your region or abroad. Some plans include more features than others, so read the fine print. For example, if you are traveling to an area with poor access to hospitals and emergency care (most places in the third world), make sure your policy will fly you home or to a nearby facility that can perform the procedures you might need in case of emergency. If you travel frequently and your policy doesn't cover you while you're abroad, you can buy separate insurance, relatively cheaply, that will fly you home if anything happens while you're abroad.

•• Finding a Doc ••

Finding a doctor can be tricky if you wait until you have a real problem. If you move to a new area or no longer feel comfortable seeing your previous physician, you will need to find a doctor. Ask around. Find a doctor who comes recommended by a friend or relative you trust. Check with your insurance company to make sure that the physician you are considering is covered by your plan. Then call the doctor's office. Keep in mind that it might take months to get a new patient appointment at some offices, so don't wait until you have a problem.

Get a checkup once a year. This helps establish your relationship with your primary doctor. If you are a woman, you might want to combine your yearly physical with a yearly gyn exam (since you should do that annually, too). Prevention goes a long way in reducing disease, so ask your doctor what steps you can take to keep yourself in great shape. One of the best ways to avoid getting sick is to wash your hands often. Also check in with your doc to make sure you're eating right and getting enough exercise, that you're up on vaccines, and that you know the risks if you're sexually active.

Go to the dentist and eye doctor, too: Flossing every day and using antiseptic mouthwash can make a huge difference in terms of the future health of your teeth and gums. But you still need to have regular checkups. Going in for a cleaning every six months reduces the likelihood that you will need an operation in the future.

Getting an annual eye exam is important because detached retinas and cataracts are relatively common. Although these are easily treated when caught early, they are a huge burden otherwise.

You have a right to feel respected and to ask questions about your care. Find a doctor who will explain diagnoses to you, who makes you feel comfortable, and whom you like. If you don't like the first doctor you visit, it's okay (and worthwhile) to change. And, even if you like your current doc, it's fine and normal to get a second opinion before undergoing any major surgery or after any life-changing diagnosis.

•• Knowing Your Health History ••

> *"I'm normally a really healthy person, but a few months ago I had pain in my chest. I hadn't seen a doctor in five years and since then I'd moved. Getting my records forwarded was a real pain, but I had to get them since I didn't know if any of my old tests were relevant to this new problem."*
>
> — Sam, 22, temp worker

Most doctor's offices keep your records for about five years and then destroy them or put them in storage or on microfilm. Therefore, it's important keep track of your own medical records. The easiest way to do this is to compile a personal health history — unless you really like microfilm.

Get a three-ring binder for easy handling in the future. File a request at your doctor's office for copies of your records. Remember to get records from all of the doctors you use, including specialists (i.e., gyn, orthopedists, psychologists, etc.). You may be charged a small fee for copies. Legally, your records belong to the doctor's office, not to you, which makes the next steps even more important.

Make a summary page for easy access that includes your name, address, phone number, and two emergency contact people. Also write down all your insurance information, such as policy numbers and contact info for the insurance companies. Compile a list of all vaccines you have received, with dates, and medications you have taken in the past. Also indicate why you took them. It is essential to know what vaccines you've had. Some are mandatory and some are not. When was the last time you had a tetanus shot? Make a list of all medications you are currently taking, and why, as well as your blood type.

List any illnesses your family members have had, such as high blood pressure, heart disease, cancer, arthritis, etc. This will help you and your doctor know if you have a predisposition to any genetic illnesses. If you can, interview your parents and grandparents to find out as much about your family medical history as possible.

Whenever you visit the doctor, bring a piece of paper and jot down the date and why you went. Ask the doctor to explain his or her diagnosis. Take note of any new medication you receive and why. If you do this each time you visit, you will have a great personal health record that will come in handy down the road and will help you understand your own body. Ask for updated copies of your records once a year (you only need copies of the new stuff) to add to your binder.

You only get one body. Take good care of it, and it will take care of you.

"When I started medical school, I was supposed to have had a hepatitis B vaccine. I couldn't remember if I had gotten one, but luckily, I had all of the information in this notebook I keep with all my health info. Most of the other students had to go through the hassle of getting records forwarded from doctors at home, but I had all my stuff right there."

— Gina, 24, student

Taking Care of
Your Home

ROOMATE NEED'D
TO SHAIR STUDEO APARTMINT

IMMEDATE NEED FOR A ROOMMATE TO SHAIR VERY, VERY SMALL STUDEO APARTMINT.
MUST BE A NON-SMOKING-VEGITARIAN-MUSICHUN, WHO LOVES CATS, HAS OWN CAR
AND LIKES TO DRIVE PEEPLE AROWND... A LOT. NEED SOME-ONE WHO HAS A TV,
PHONE, BED, COUCH, KICHEN STUFF, WEARS A SIZE 6 AND LIKES TO SHAIR.

INTRESTED, PLEES CALL 555-1234.

MUST BE ABLE TO MOOV IN RIGHT AWAY, AND HELP OUT WITH 3 MONTHS OF BACK RENT!!

CALL LUZ ZERR
555-1234

CALL LUZ ZERR
555-1234

CALL LUZ ZERR
555-1234

CALL LUZ ZERR
555-1234

CALL LUZ ZERR
555-1234

CALL LUZ ZERR
555-1234

CALL LUZ ZERR
555-1234

CALL LUZ ZERR
555-1234

CALL LUZ ZERR
555-1234

CALL LUZ ZERR
555-1234

CALL LUZ ZERR
555-1234

CALL LUZ ZERR
555-1234

FINDING A PLACE TO LIVE
•• Hunting for Housing and Housemates ••

Give yourself as much time as possible to find a new home, and when you do leave your old place, save yourself some money by fixing and cleaning anything your landlord might use as an excuse to keep your security deposit.

To find a new home, there are several places to begin your search, including the newspaper and local websites. To find such a website, type the name of your town and housing or rentals or apartments (whatever you're looking for) into a search engine. Many towns and cities have sites devoted to individuals and groups who are looking for housing — sometimes you can even look for roommates on these sites. You should also let all your friends and family in the area know that you are looking. They may know people who want to rent out a room or people who know people... you get the point. Walk around a neighborhood where you'd like to live. Some people save money by skipping expensive ads in the newspaper and simply putting a sign in their window. Knock on doors and ask if anyone knows of houses that will soon be available.

Figure out how much you can pay. Account for extra costs, such as utility bills and small repairs you will need to make yourself. Living with housemates will allow you to get a bigger, possibly nicer place for your money and will also help distribute the cost of utilities, cleaning supplies, and other household expenses.

When looking for housemates, however, beware. Do you like to go to bed early when you have work the next morning? Does it drive you nuts when people don't wash their dishes right away? Does your prospective roommate have a pet that sheds? On the other hand, do you like to stay up late, wait days before doing dishes, and have the most adorable puppy ever? Will any of this bother your housemates? Sit down and have a serious discussion with any potential housemates about your living styles. Make sure that you are in agreement about house rules *before* you sign a lease. Also consider any significant others. (Does your best friend's significant other drive you nuts? You might end up effectively living with both of them.)

•• Questions to Ask ••

Once you have housemates and a price range, look at places that fit your needs. Talk to current tenants. Ask if they like the landlord. Find out why or why not. Ask if the landlord is prompt in making repairs and if there are any major problems associated with the house. Do the toilets leak? Does everything in the kitchen work? Is garbage pickup included? Who pays for it? Will they take recycling? Ask about average utility bills, too. What type of heat does the place use? How much does it usually cost in the winter? Are you responsible for a water bill? Reconfirm all this information with the landlord.

> **It is a good idea** to make friends with current tenants in houses you are considering leasing, since they will not only have information you want, but may also have furniture to leave behind that you could buy for peanuts. Once you've decided to take the place, ask them for the phone numbers of the gas and electric companies they use. If you do not inform utility companies in advance that you are the new account holder, they will cancel service when the old occupants move out, leaving you without hot water and lights for several days. If you call in advance, the transition should be smooth.

•• Signing a Lease ••

Once you find a place you like, settle any questions before signing a lease. Use your best judgment. If anything in the lease seems unclear or dangerous, ask the landlord to clarify. If you are not satisfied, look it over with a lawyer. It is also reasonable to ask the landlord to make repairs before you move in. Have each specific agreement written into the lease. You can ask for an inspection by a professional such as a plumber or electrician if anything seems fishy, although you may have to pay for this yourself. Ask for anything that seems within reason (storm windows to lower your heating bill, a new refrigerator if the old one is on its last legs, plumbing issues, and so on).

Once you decide you want the place you will likely be asked to put down a security deposit (usually one month's rent), as well as the first and last months' rents. To protect your deposit, make a list of all damages (nicks on walls, faulty faucets, etc.), and give a copy to the landlord. This way you will not be charged for existing damages when you move out.

Strike a bargain. Sometimes after you give the landlord a list of what needs to be done, you can bargain — offer to fix stuff in exchange for lower rent. Offer to paint if certain rooms need it or to fix up the deck. If you decide to do this, make sure that the agreement is spelled out in writing — i.e., "Tenant will paint living room and dining room in return for $200 off of August's rent. Landlord will pay for all materials at cost documented by receipts." This deal will save you some money and ensure that the job gets done.

When signing a lease, remember that you have certain rights as a tenant and it is your landlord's legal responsibility to uphold a baseline level of habitability. If the house, room, or apartment you are considering does not meet basic safety standards, think about looking elsewhere. However, if you are already living there, you have two options. You can either ask your landlord to do the repairs necessary to make the place livable, or you can do them yourself and deduct the cost from your rent. If you decide to do the repairs without the help from management, make sure to save all the receipts for materials and to log any time you spend on the project. Avoid doing structural repairs on your own (i.e., don't go smashing holes in your wall to create an airier atmosphere), and ask for help with any job where you might make the situation worse (fixing electronics or your fridge). If your landlord does not respond to your needs in a timely manner, consider sending a certified letter listing your complaints.

If you like your space and don't want to leave when your lease ends, you may have the right to up to a full year of month-to-month leasing. Talk to your landlord as far in advance as you can (once you know you want to stay). If you have been a good tenant, he or she will be very happy to keep you, and you should be able to negotiate to keep your rent the same (which can be a big advantage against inflation).

If, on the other hand, you want to leave before the term of your lease is up, you should know that while you are technically liable for the full term of the lease, it is also the landlord's responsibility to make "every effort" to find a new tenant once you have given notice that you want to leave. Again, give as much notice as possible and if your landlord can't find someone, consider subletting.

LIVING WITH OTHERS
•• Paying Bills ••

To make sure that everyone pays on time, it is a good idea to set up a common bank account that is separate from everyone's personal accounts. Before you move in together, appoint a treasurer who will have access to the account, and ask everyone to deposit the same amount (say $200). Set an amount that everyone will contribute each month, and then pay bills from this account. This system allows for some flexibility — if there is money in the account to begin with, a few people's late payments won't cause mayhem in the house. The treasurer will still need to be vigilant about collecting, but having one central account will definitely eliminate some of the stress.

•• Dividing Bills ••

Another way to avoid bill hassles is to divide the utilities under different people's names. Make one person responsible for the phone and cable, another for the electric, and another for the gas. Having a bill in his or her name will make each housemate more likely to attend to at least one bill.

Keep all house bills and receipts in a common folder so that accounting is accessible to the whole house. If you are the treasurer, keep a detailed account of each time someone pays you and each time you write a check on behalf of the house.

> **Sign separate leases** when moving in with several
> roommates. Ask your landlord to sign an agreement
> with each occupant individually. That way, if one
> person doesn't pay or moves to China, you won't be
> held responsible. Some landlords will accommodate
> this request and some will not, but it is definitely worth
> asking about.

•• Subletting ••

If your boss offers you the opportunity to go to Barbados for
three months on business, but you can't afford to pay for housing
there *and* keep up with your current rent, you should sublet. Most
leases allow you to rent out your room while you are away, as long
as you take responsibility for paying the landlord directly and for
any trouble caused by your sublessee. With this in mind, choose your
stand-in carefully. It is wise to make a copy of your lease in which
you change the language from "landlord"/"tenant" to "sublettor"/
"occupant," and to have your sublessee sign it. This gives him or her
a chance to see what rules you have agreed to with your landlord
and requires that he or she abide by the same. Make sure that the
sublessee understands any specific rules. For example, if you have
neighbors who don't like noise, don't sublet to a rock band that
wants to practice in the garage. Ask him or her for a security deposit
and for the first month's rent as well. If you feel at all unsure, it is
reasonable to ask for references. Determine a system of payment
so that you will be able to get the money while you're away. If it
is a relatively short period (say, three months), you might just ask
for the whole amount up front. Having to chase people around later
stinks.

If you're having trouble finding someone to take your place, consider lowering the rent a bit. It is better to lose a little money while you're away than to have the room left empty with you footing the whole bill. Advertise in a local paper and on local housing websites (most colleges have housing databases) and tell your friends that you're looking for renters. An added bonus to finding a friend of a friend is that you will have an automatic reference.

CLEANING

> *"I hate cleaning, but doing a little at a time helps."*
> — Jack, 23, grad student

I know you don't want to read this section. There aren't many people who truly enjoy cleaning. If you live with housemates, share or rotate these duties. Cleaning regularly will make your home more pleasant than leaving it for months. When using cleaning products, wear rubber gloves because these products can be irritating and sometimes downright dangerous. Read the label before using any strong product since the vapors from mixing certain ones can be fatal.

•• Odors ••

If you've picked up all your dirty laundry and taken all of last weekend's dirty dishes to the kitchen, but your room still smells funny, chances are that the odor may reside in the carpet or in your shoes. If you're athletic, keep your smelly shoes and gear in the hall outside. If you suspect the carpet, sprinkle baking soda all over the carpet area and let it sit for about 15 minutes. Then vacuum it up. Also try leaving the windows open for half an hour to air out the stale smells.

•• Stains ••

For stains on the carpet and elsewhere, first try to avoid making them. When you do spill something, pour club soda on the area right away. Then soak it up with a rag or paper towels. Always dab — never rub. If that doesn't work, check *The Super Stain Remover Book* by Jack Cassimatis. Yes, this book actually exists and will help you find out what will remove your particular stain. There are also several comprehensive websites dedicated to this topic. Go to a search engine and search for "stain removal" and the staining substance.

•• Sinks ••

Clear toothbrushes, soap bottles, and anything else off the sink. Apply a cleaning product, such as bathroom bubbles or sink cleaner, and let it sit for ten minutes. Wipe the cleaner off and scrub any leftover gunk with a sponge (use the abrasive side for tough stuff). Using the sponge, rinse the sink with water.

•• Tubs ••

Wet the tub with water from the shower and let it drain so that the surface is wet but not holding water. Sprinkle tub and tile cleaner (disinfectant with bleach) on the wet areas and let it sit for at least ten minutes. Scrub the tub with a sponge, and rinse it several times with the shower or with cups of water. Make sure to rinse it especially well if you plan to take a bath. If you have brown stains on the tub, your culprit is likely hard water. Hard-water stain removers are available at hardware stores. Strong cleaners are good for the tub, but bad for your skin. Make sure to wear gloves (and don't use these gloves for anything related to food or washing dishes) and open a window for fresh air while you scrub.

"I like scrubbing the tub. I find it meditative."
— Brett, 22, mathematician

•• Toilets ••

Buy a toilet cleaner in a bottle with a tilted head for ease in reaching up under the rim. Spray or squirt cleaner around the inside rim of the toilet in the bowl. Let it sit for ten to fifteen minutes, then scrub with a toilet brush. Flush. Repeat if necessary. If you don't have a toilet brush, buy one — it will make toilet cleaning much more manageable. Also make sure you own a plunger, just in case.

•• Floors ••

Most of the time, sweeping is enough to pick up hair and dust from the floor. In the bathroom, though, mop every other week to avoid scum buildup. Water sloshing around from the shower and sink can lead to little colonies of bacteria if you aren't careful.

REPAIRS

When you moved in, they told you the house had "charm." However, you've discovered that by "charm" they meant a fussy drain, prissy toilets, and a pest welcoming committee. The positive news is that dealing with these types of problems "builds character." You can probably fix more than you'd think, but unless you're Mickey Mouse, the brooms won't be doing any cleaning or fixing on their own.

•• Clogged Drains ••

This is likely something you can fix yourself. In the bathroom, hair is the biggest clogging offender. To prevent clogs, remove any hair from the drain right after you shower or use the sink. Drain-freeing chemicals are a reasonable solution if your drain is only slightly clogged (water is draining more slowly than usual), but if your sink is stopped all the way, be aware that these chemicals are powerful and work by eating the clogging culprit. They can also eat your pipes if left sitting too long. These chemicals are bad for the environment and your skin. If you choose to use them, make sure to wear gloves, and be cautious about performing any of the following repairs after having dumped them in.

If the clog is too serious for a liquid drain cleaner, first remove the stopper or strainer (the thing that is supposed to catch your engagement ring so you don't lose it). That said, also remove any jewelry and small objects sitting close to the sink that you don't want to lose down the drain. Clean the strainer. Next get a wire hanger and unbend it to make an unclogging tool. Stick it down the drain and feel around to dislodge whatever scuzz is causing the blockage. Pull out all that you can and push the rest down. If you know what is clogging the drain (i.e., you dropped a fork down there while doing dishes), consider sticking pliers into the darkness to retrieve the culprit.

If this doesn't work, try plunging. Seal off your overflow hole with a wet rag. Run enough water to cover the bulb of the plunger (or use the water that has built up due to the clog). Put the plunger over the drain to create a seal (going in at a diagonal helps get as much air as possible out from the plunger cup). Once sealed, pump up and down with the plunger handle as forcefully as you can. Expect to work for several minutes. Remove the plunger once in a while to check your progress. If it's working, you'll hear a sucking sound as stuff starts to go down. If not, keep trying.

If neither of these techniques works, you will have to remove the plug, which consists of a screw in the U-shaped pipe under the sink. If we're talking about your tub, you may need a professional. Make sure to put a bucket under the plug before you open it since water will probably flow out. Stick your hanger tool up toward the drain and see if you can free the clog from this end.

In *none* of this works, the trap will need to be removed. Ask a professional or competent friend for help.

•• Clogged Toilets ••

First of all, as tempting as it is to try flushing again when the water starts rising, resist the urge. Flushing again will only add more water to the problem, making it more likely that the toilet will overflow. Unless you like overflowing toilets — in which case you should see a therapist — don't flush again.

That said, the best way to deal with a clogged toilet is to plunge. Most people keep their plunger near the toilet (and so should you, since it is embarrassing to have to leave the crime scene and go find this piece of equipment). Make a seal over the drain and plunge for a minute or so at a time. Check periodically to see if it's working. Be persistent and hope this works: the next option is even less pleasant.

If this doesn't work, unwind a hanger and poke to dislodge the offending materials. Making an "L" with the end of the hanger will let you pull in addition to poking (which helps), but beware of scratching the porcelain. Sometimes a combination of hanger poking and plunging will do the trick better than either method alone.

•• Leaky Toilets ••

If your toilet runs, it may be that the level of the floating bob needs to be manually lifted to stop water flow. Take off the top of the toilet tank and lift the arm. The water should stop running (and don't worry, the water up there is totally clean). If the problem is persistent or consists of leakage elsewhere, watch the parts move as you flush. See if any part is obviously broken. If so, take it out and replace that part. This is cheaper than calling a professional. If you can't figure it out yourself, call a plumber.

•• Shower Curtains ••

If your shower curtain has lots of little spots that are really hard to clean off then it can get moldy. To eliminate this problem, first try your washing machine. (Take the curtain down and wash it with half a cup of baking soda and some bleach as disinfectant. Make sure to get it out before the spin cycle.) Another option is to clean it manually. Fill a bucket with a diluted bleach solution (see the bottle for proportions), and find a pair of rubber gloves and a sponge. Sponge the bleach solution onto the curtain and let it sit for several minutes before washing it off. This should do the trick (even if it doesn't remove all the spots, it will disinfect the surface). If not, you can buy special mildew and shower cleaners. To prevent this is the first place, clean the curtain regularly and always leave spread out to dry (with no creases where mold could incubate). If you have a glass door, buy a squeegee — using it after each shower will save a lot of time in the long run.

•• Dishwasher Problems ••

If your dishwasher smells like smoke during the drying cycle, something is probably resting against the heater that dries the dishes. Stop the washer. The heater is either on the top or the bottom, so find it and see if something is against it. If so, take it out.

If food remains on the plates after they're finished in the machine, start pre-rinsing your dishes before loading them. Make sure to get all the big chunks off. Don't let food dry onto your dishes since this cements the crud and makes it harder for the dishwasher to do its job. Make it a habit to rinse dishes and put them in the dishwasher immediately, rather than letting them pile up in the sink. This will keep fruit flies away, too.

Never put wood in the dishwasher (this goes for wooden knives, spoons, and bowls) unless you like splinters. It is also a good idea to hand wash knives since you will want to dry them right away to prevent corrosion and dulling. Keeping wood out of the dishwasher will also help avoid overheating.

If you have streaky dishes, you may have hard water or you may need to switch detergents. If it is the former, learn to love the streaks because softening all the water in your house would be a big and expensive project. To determine if you are lucky and it's the latter, first try using less detergent. If that doesn't work, try other brands. It's tempting to use more detergent, but that hurts the machine.

•• Pests ••

If your home has a bug problem, you may be able to deal with it yourself. Call in a professional if you suspect carpenter ants or termites. These critters eat through the structure of your house and usually leave little piles of sawdust, tunnels, cracks, or peeling paint where the floor meets the wall; other telltale signs include hollow sounds when you tap beams or a lot of flying insects. You can usually hear carpenter ants munching on the beams — they're not subtle.

Before you call a professional, make sure your house is extra clean (no food lying out to temp pests) and try a few commercial pest killers. When using sprays or traps, focus on areas near doors, windows, and the wall-floor intersections, but keep poison out of the reach of pets.

The cup trick: If you see an individual bug and are nice enough not to want to kill it but not nice enough to want to share your living space with it, get a cup and a piece of paper. Put the cup over the bug to trap it, and then slide the paper underneath. This will trap the bug temporarily. Fold the sides of the paper so that you can hold it securely over the cup opening and walk the creature outside. Remove the paper and the bug can go free.

If you have spiders and are not getting bitten, consider letting them stay. They eat other bugs, especially flies, and are often harmless.

If you have mice, mousetraps come in all varieties but they usually have some really unpleasant component. You might have to kill the mouse or deal with a live mouse. Another solution is to buy a box of warfrin, which is sold under various trade names, but is basically a blood thinner. Leave it open where mice can get it. After ingesting it, mice become very thirsty, go outside, gorge themselves on water, and die. This is good because you don't have to deal with them. If you have pets or children, however, *do not* use this method, since it will poison them as well. Another note of caution if you choose this method: don't leave standing water in the sink since the mice will go there to die.

•• Hanging Pictures ••

The key to hanging a picture securely is finding a stud. (This term refers either to the wood frame that runs behind your sheetrock wall to give it support, or the handsome guy who'll find it for you.) Find the stud by knocking along the wall. When you come to a place that sounds less hollow than the rest of the wall, make a little pencil dot. Since studs usually run vertically, you can hang your picture anywhere on this vertical line. Stick a nail or a screw where you want to hang the picture, but remember to account for the location of the fastener on the back of the frame. The nail or screw will probably be a few inches below the top of the final image. If this sounds like a pain and you have a little extra cash, you can buy picture hangers, which can hang relatively heavy loads without needing a stud. Also, they are kinder to the walls and leave less of a mark.

Getting Dressed

THE CLOTHES
•• Dressing in Style Without Going Broke ••

Getting dressed can be a real drag when you haven't done laundry and don't like your wardrobe that much to begin with. Buying fashionable clothing, however, can take its toll on your wallet — trends change so quickly. Maybe you want to set the trends yourself: buy a pack of garbage bags and call it "chic modern." If that's not your thing, here are some tips on how you can stay hot without breaking your bank.

- ✔ Buy simple pieces that won't go out of style, and then accessorize. If everyone is wearing something trendy, but the only reason you'd wear it is to fit in, skip it. A cool necklace or belt matched with simple basics is as stylish, and cheaper, than a whole new outfit.

- ✔ Choose flattering pieces over trendy ones. If you want to look good, you have to feel good about the way you look. Choosing pieces that fit your body type will help you feel better than going for something in style that doesn't suit you.

- ✔ Look in the newspaper or online for special sales and coupons. You may be surprised at what you find. If there's a two-for-one sale happening, go in with a friend and you'll both get one at half price!

- ✔ Shop in outlets. Most big companies have outlets to sell the items they didn't sell the previous year. Some stores don't change product lines that much, so the stuff from last year is basically the same as this year's, only at half the price or less. This is especially true for simple clothing lines.

✓ Trade clothes with your friends. When you're sick of your wardrobe, take out everything you don't want and ask your friends to do the same. Then have a party to swap. Your trash may be your friend's treasure.

✓ Trust your instincts when developing a personal style. Chances are you'll look your best if you feel good about what you're wearing; don't let other people boss you around. Choose clothes that make you feel great about yourself, and your confidence will carry you.

> *"Looking good is all about confidence, but how can you look confident if you can't even walk comfortably?"*
> — Jan, 30, designer

✓ When buying dress shoes or work shoes, be picky and only buy comfortable footwear. Also, be open to buying shoes when you run across a great sale or a pair you particularly love, even though you may not be in the market for them.

✓ Buy quality instead of quantity. No one will notice if you wear the same black skirt or pants more than once in the same week. Pay extra for things that will last and be comfortable. Buy one suit, for example, and three shirts/ties to mix and match or blouses/belts/jewelry that go with it to change the look.

✔ Think about how easy it is to move around in the garment you're considering. Before you buy it, always sit down in the outfit to see how it looks when you're seated.

✔ Learn how to tie a tie (see illustration).

•• Taking Care of Your Clothes ••

✔ Sew your own buttons back on. Buy a needle and thread and sew in and out of the holes and through the fabric until the button is secure. Use a thread color that is similar to the button or the fabric of the clothing if you want it to blend in, or use a bright color if you want to show off that you did it yourself. Sewing the button too tightly will make it difficult to squeeze the button through the hole. Sew your button loosely, then when the needle is between the button and the fabric, wrap the thread around itself several times to secure the button and to make a buffer. A good trick to make this easier is to criss-cross two pins underneath the button while sewing. They will ensure that just the right amount of space is left between the button and the fabric, making it easier to wrap the extra thread.

✔ When washing clothes, wait until all the water is in the machine and agitating to add bleach. Use dryer sheets in the dryer to make your clothes more pliant, which helps them last longer.

Clothes Washing Tips from My Grandma:
Did you ever notice that all garments have cleaning instructions and many say, "dry clean only"? Most of the time, the "dry clean only" label is inserted simply to protect the manufacturer since so many consumers are careless when washing their clothes; they use harsh detergents, scalding water, or toss garments into the dryer without thinking.

Don't be naive... if an item is 100% cotton, examine it carefully to make sure there are no shoulder pads or other reasons to take the warning seriously. If it's just plain cotton, don't be afraid to wash it. But do so carefully — cool water, no wringing, and gently shape the garment when you lay it down on a towel or hang it on a hanger. The same thing goes for rayon.

Some special clothes, especially if they are black or silk, do better with dry cleaning. Always check the care tags and be sure not to dry clean clothes that say "do not dry clean" since the dry cleaning process will ruin them — and you'll still have to pay for it.

✓ Instead of taking your clothes to the dry cleaner, try dry cleaning bags for your dryer. They're cheaper than a professional and work pretty well. Hang the clothes to dry afterward and air out the smell of the chemicals.

✓ When ironing, remember: choose the heat setting on the iron based on fabric type (listed on the garment's tag). Turn the garment inside out and test the iron on a seam to make sure nothing burns or gets discolored. Leave the garment inside out while you iron to avoid ironing stains. For pants and skirts, do the pleats first. Iron the hem and then work your way up. On a dress shirt, do the back panel (called the apron) first. For all clothing, lay the piece flat and smooth it with your hand, then run the iron over it with even strokes. Never leave the iron sitting on one place for more than a few seconds since that will burn the fabric and ruin your clothing. When you are finished with the hot iron and have unplugged it, move it to a non-flammable spot where it won't get knocked over or walked into because it will take a while to cool off.

If you don't feel like ironing, a good alternative is to throw your wrinkled clothing in the dryer with a damp, clean towel. The steam will smooth out the wrinkles. Make sure to take your clothes out right away after they're done, though, because if you leave them in the dryer, they'll wrinkle again.

•• Treating Stains ••

In general, it is best to treat stains as soon as possible before they set. Also, follow instructions on any piece of clothing (disregard the advice below if your shirt says "dry clean only," for example). Here are some of the most common fixes.

If you're wearing white and you spill something on yourself, wet the stain and spray a small amount of bleach-based household cleaner on it. Then rinse the area right away.

Red fruits and juices. First, stretch the part of the fabric with the stain on it over a bowl in the sink. Then pour boiling water on the stain from about a foot above the material. The results are amazing.

Wash the garment in the warmest water possible, using a non-soap detergent (natural soaps can make the stain more permanent). If this doesn't work, test a spot on the inseam to see if your garment is bleach-safe. If it is, try bleaching out the stain.

Coffee. Pretreat the stain with stain stick or spray and heavy detergent, and then launder as directed. If this doesn't work, try bleaching.

Blood. Use cold water to remove the crusty surface junk and as much of the stain as possible. Do not use hot water! Then, soak the material in about a quart of cool water mixed with a teaspoon of detergent and a tablespoon of ammonia. Do this in a well-ventilated area since the gas released from mixing some chemicals can be dangerous or deadly if you breathe in too much. Let this mixture sit for about half an hour, rubbing the stained garment gently once in a while to loosen the stain. If this procedure does not remove the stain, you can try a little bit of hydrogen peroxide before putting detergent on it as you're about to wash it. Do not leave hydrogen peroxide on the clothes thinking that longer may work better — it will eat holes in the fabric. Rinse it with cool water to remove the hydrogen peroxide before washing the garment.

Chewing gum. Try freezing the gum. If it's on clothing, stick the whole garment in the freezer. If it's on carpet or something else you can't directly freeze, use an ice cube to harden the gum. Once it has hardened, you should be able to peel the gum off or shatter it and then scrape it off with a dull knife.

Pen ink. Try using some isopropyl rubbing alcohol. First blot the ink away with a paper towel. Next dab on some alcohol and blot with towels. If the stain is big, take off the garment and pour alcohol on the reverse side of the fabric. Blot with towels. If this doesn't work, try presoaking it with detergent and washing it on the hottest setting allowed for your fabric. This probably won't work for permanent ink. Instead, try washing the garment immediately with hot water and then consult a dry cleaner or use a commercial dye stripper. Sometimes, hairspray also works on pen ink.

Oil. Pretreat the stain with a stain stick or spray. Let this set, then pretreat it again with the heaviest laundry detergent safe for your fabric. Wash it on hot. If this doesn't work, try bleaching. If you don't want to buy any of these products, try pouring some milk on the stain. Let it sit for several minutes then wash it out. Make sure to remove all the milk, or your clothing will smell sour.

THE HAIR
•• Getting a Good Cut ••

Q: Where is the best place to get a haircut?
A: On your head.

Your head is one of the first parts of your body that people see and judge. This means that your hairstyle is important. Here are some tips for getting the look you want.

✔ Take pictures of old haircuts you have liked on yourself to a barber or stylist. Try to avoid envisioning your new haircut in terms of celebrity 'dos ("I want layers like Jennifer Aniston") because chances are you have a different facial structure and hair type than your chosen celebrity. The same cut will look different on you.

✔ Talk to your stylist as he or she cuts your hair. If you're worried that your hair is getting shorter than you might like, say so before it's too late.

•• Cutting Your Own Hair ••

Q: How do I cut my own hair?
A: Very carefully. With scissors.

Cutting your own hair helps to avoid communication errors. It can be difficult to explain what you want to a stylist, and doing it yourself eliminates the need for explanation. Now you're probably thinking, "Oh my gosh, how do you do the back? I could never cut my own hair." But never fear, it is easier than you think. It's also faster and cheaper than making an appointment, schlepping down to the shop, and then waiting to get a cut that doesn't totally satisfy you.

> *"I save over $1,000 each year by cutting, coloring, and perming my hair at home."*
>
> — Sharon, 20, disc jockey

✔ Find a spot with good light and a wall mirror (you'll also need a hand mirror to look at the back).

✔ Get your hair wet, then towel dry so you're not dripping.

✔ Put down newspaper for easier cleanup.

Long Hair

✔ If your hair is long, use clips to pin up all but the undermost layer (leave about an inch row on the scalp down — see Fig. 2). Then trim the basic shape you are going for. Let down rows (about an inch each) one at a time and trim, leaving each layer a tiny bit longer than the last. Go slowly — you can always cut more, but growing hair back takes time. Once you have the basic shape you are going for (i.e., each section is the length you want it to be), you can either leave it (for a straight, blunt cut), or you can add layers.

Fig. 2: For a blunt cut.

✔ To add layers, hold up a column about one inch wide from your part to your neck (see Fig. 3), and cut straight along your fingers. Work your way around your head in one-inch columns. This leaves the individual pieces of hair the same length, but the hair higher on your scalp will appear shorter.

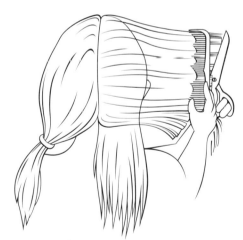

Fig. 3: For layers.

✔ For the back, I often ask a friend for help. It can be tough to work with two mirrors (it's not as intuitive as you might think). Explain *exactly* what you want your friend to do and how you want it done. I usually hold the hair myself and ask them to cut along my fingers since I have a better sense of where my fingers are than where the blades are.

Short Hair

✔ Cutting short hair can be tougher than cutting long hair. I like to use a lot of layers for short hair. One easy way to get a good short cut is to follow the steps for making layers above, and apply this method to the entire head. This works best for fine hair because if your hair has too much body to begin with, shorter layers on top may start to spike.

> **Leave more hair in the front** than you think you need. You can always trim more, and the area around your face is the most critical.

✔ Plan beforehand. Think about exactly what you want the cut to end up looking like, and then err on the longer side. Remember that hair shrinks a little when it dries.

✔ Again, consider asking a friend to help with the back.

✔ If you're feeling doubtful about the job you've just done, wait a day or two. Sometimes after a shampoo, or with fresh eyes, the cut will look better. If you're still not satisfied, you can always go to a professional to clean it up. For this reason, when you first start out as your own barber, leave your hair longer than you want it to end up, and go shorter as you gain confidence.

Taking Care of Business

CHOOSING A CAREER
•• Finding a Job That's Right for You ••

Ask yourself the following questions:

If I could do whatever I wanted, what would it be?

Make a list of things you love to do. Make another list of things that you do well. Where do these lists overlap? If you love talking to people and are really good at convincing them to do what you want, think about a job in sales. If you are always organizing what to do with your friends when you go out, think about a job involving management skills. If you are shy but know a lot about computers, think about a job involving information technology. If the only two things on your list of things you love to do are "eating ice cream," and "watching sitcoms," you should rewrite the list, being a little more open-minded — or get a job scooping. If you choose the second option, cross "having an expensive house/car/ vacation" off the list of things you love.

What job is right for me?

Consider what you like to do along with factors such as location, your level of education or training, and how far into the future you are willing to commit. For example, would you rather live in a city or a more rural area? Do you plan to go back to school in the future? If you want a job that requires a PhD, you might need to think about getting a part-time job to help pay your bills while you apply to schools. If you want an MBA, however, consider applying for jobs that offer you the opportunity to work while you get your degree. Many companies will pay for masters degrees, especially business degrees, so it's a good idea to get a job and work a little before applying to an MBA program.

What contacts do I have?

Maybe a family friend does something that sounds interesting to you, or maybe you are friendly with your grocer who knows a customer in your field of choice. Ask around and don't be afraid to use the people you know. Ask them to introduce you to people who do things that interest you, or to put in a good word for you. If you are lucky enough to know people who do interesting things and you can get in touch with them, ask them how they got into their businesses. Find out what they like and don't like about their jobs. If the conversation goes well, they might offer to introduce you to someone who's hiring. If you tell lots of friends what you think you want to do, they can keep their ears open and let you know when jobs are up for grabs.

How much do I really need to make?

The more flexible you are with your salary, the pickier you can afford to be both in terms of what jobs you'll take and how soon you need to find one. For example, if you are fresh out of school and don't have much experience, most employers won't be jumping to throw cash your way. If, however, you can afford to work for free, or for very little, you can intern with a company that will teach you the tricks of the trade and you will gain the experience needed to land a paying job. If this is not an option (most of us *do* need to make money), don't despair. If you are serious about the low-paying job experience, you might consider a less attractive, part-time job that will pay the bills until you have the experience you need for the career you want.

How can I make myself useful to people in power?

If you are currently in school, make friends with professors. Stay in touch with them after you graduate. They were once students too, and might have advice when you are choosing a career. If you are currently in a job situation that you hate, don't burn bridges.

In fact, try to make friends with people in power who will give references when you apply for your next job.

> *"If one has something to offer, one should offer it; I'm good at programming, and I'm good at managing people... so I program for research, and I manage people as a head teaching assistant... and as a result, there are professors here who can really vouch for me. I don't think it was a deliberate decision on my part, but making myself useful to people in power has had a substantial effect on my job prospects and general 'marketability' as a grad student or employee. And it was fun."*
> — Ben, 21, computer science major

If you don't know what you want to do, talk to everyone you meet about what they do. When what they do interests you, ask how they ended up where they are and if they know anyone in their field who might be hiring.

If you don't find the ideal job right away, think about the benefits of a less-than-ideal job. This isn't a permanent commitment. You can change jobs later if you don't find the perfect one now, and if you need to pay rent, that second option might start looking pretty good.

What would you look for if you were hiring?

Volunteer for a local organization and try to get on a committee that does hiring. This way, you'll see what looks good on a resume and what is less desirable.

> *"Always make friends with secretaries and janitors.*
> *They can make a tremendous difference."*
> — Katherine, 50, workforce veteran

•• Getting the Job You Want ••

Once you've found a great job prospect, do your homework. Find out as much as you can about the company. What have they done that is impressive? What questions do you want answered? What do they need that you could fulfill? Most companies publish an annual report that you can probably find online. If you can't find it on the web, ask to have one sent to you. Look for the strengths and weaknesses of the company. Find out about any recent changes in management. Know as much as you can about the company before your interview.

Before the interview, make a list of things you are really good at. Think about what will make you a strong candidate for the job. Then don't be afraid to tell your potential employer about your attributes. If the job is advertised, you most likely will have competition. If you are asked to submit an application or resume, include a cover letter explaining why you want the job and what you would bring to the position. Be thoughtful in this letter. Do not say that you are only looking for a pit stop on your road to success or that you just really need the money or that one of your parents suggested you go for the job. If these are your reasons, consider framing them differently: "I look forward to potentially working with your company since I believe I have something to offer and I can learn a considerable amount, too." Make sure your spelling is correct. Check your grammar. Have a teacher, friend, or parent read your resume and cover letter before you send it in. This will help catch thoughtless mistakes and verify that what you've written makes sense. It is crucial that your application be technically flawless.

Think about what sets you apart and what your employer will see. For example, if you are applying for a job as a wait person at a fancy restaurant, make sure you look clean and presentable when you drop off your application. Even if this is not the time of your interview, you may see your potential boss, and you don't want to look like someone who would contaminate the food. If you know which person is the boss, make a point of introducing yourself. Say that you are dropping off an application and you look forward to meeting him or her again in your interview. Smile. Act like someone who will bring business to the restaurant.

Make sure to practice your interview *beforehand*. Write down questions you think you might be asked and give them to a friend or family member. Prepare answers to questions such as: "Tell me about yourself," "Why do you want to work here?" "What would you bring to our business?" and "I see you have been out of work for some time. Please explain." Have your friend pretend to be the interviewer and answer each question as if it were the real thing. After you've finished, ask for feedback about your answers and presentation. This practice round will help you feel more at ease during the real interview and allow you to work out the kinks in your delivery. Some people suggest going on practice interviews before the one that is most important to you. Schedule interviews for jobs you are less interested in first so you are in the groove for the interview you really want to score.

Be prepared for unusual interviewing techniques or random questions like, "If you could be any fruit, which would it be and why?" Potential employers will often ask candidates to describe their strengths and weaknesses. Be careful on the weaknesses. Remember it is an interview and pick something that an employer would view as an asset rather than a professional liability: "I have trouble stopping sometimes. When I get into a project, I can't put it down until I'm sure it's done. I have to make sure I sleep enough when that happens."

If you are applying for a white-collar job, perhaps you can walk by the company office in advance to get an idea of how your bosses dress. People are most comfortable when others look like they do.

•• Interviews ••

During an interview, wear something clean and comfortable, but a step up from what you might usually wear. A good rule is to try to look like an employee at the company or even a little nicer — unless the employees wear suits and ties, in which case there's no need to wear a tux. Wear something that you feel confident in — for example, I'd never wear something brand-new since I feel most confident when I know exactly how I look. If everyone in the office wears polo shirts and khakis to work, wear a shirt and tie if you are a man, or nice slacks or a skirt, along with a nice shirt if you are a woman. If you are applying for a job at a gas station, forget the tie.

When you meet your potential boss, look him or her in the eye with your head up and shoulders back, shake hands (firmly but don't crush bones), smile, and use his or her name: "Nice to meet you, Dr. Henderson." Always err on the side of being too formal by using Mr., Ms., or Dr., rather than being too informal by using a first name.

The person who asks the questions controls the conversation. Prepare some questions prior to the interview, such as "Could you please describe a typical day on this job?" Also be prepared to respond to the interviewer's questions with examples of things you do well that will support your candidacy for the job. Whenever possible, use specific examples of things you have accomplished that relate to the work you will do: "In the management course I took last fall, my group had the most successful outcome for the stock market simulation." Or even better: "During my internship last summer, I was given the responsibility of interviewing a set of patients and entering the data into an Access database. What type of database software do you use here?"

Answer questions truthfully, but don't be afraid to pause and think before you speak. Take a moment to consider each question. What information is he or she looking for? You might be asked why you want the job. Use this as an opportunity to sell yourself. Tell why you think you have the skills to do the job well. Be as specific as possible. ("I'm especially interested in your new customer service initiative. I love working with people and I think it's exciting that I might have the opportunity put those skills to use with your company.") Try to connect with your interviewer. If there is a fishing magazine on his or her desk and you love to fish, mention it ("Oh, do you fish? Where do you like to go? Do you prefer worms or lures as bait?") If you make a personal connection, he or she is more likely to remember you and you are more likely to get the job.

Chances are you may be asked how much money you want to make. If you have the opportunity, throw the question back and ask what the job offers. If you answer first, you might significantly shortchange yourself. For example, you might say that you want to make X dollars. If you wait, you might discover that they are offering $2X. If you go first and are low, they will go with that figure, of course.

At the end of the interview, be prepared with questions — it shows you are interested and have done your homework. This is one of the most important parts of the interview. Showing extra interest can make the difference between getting the job and being unemployed. Reference material you read about the business and use this opportunity to make suggestions about how your participation would benefit the company. Find out the interviewer's thinking on the next steps in the hiring process, the timetable, and the process for a decision. After you leave, follow up with a thank-you note for the interview, or if appropriate, call the next day to thank your interviewer for his or her time. Say that you enjoyed your interview and ask if it would be appropriate for you to check back in a week or two.

> *"Personal contact matters a lot. I try to be objective when interviewing candidates, but if I connect with someone, if I feel comfortable with them, they're more likely to get the job."*
>
> — Selinda, 44, personnel director

Once you've been offered a job, consider what benefits it provides. Will you get health insurance? Dental? How much vacation can you take? Do other workers like the boss? Avoid jobs where the boss is universally disliked. Even if you are great with people and think you could be different, if other people have a hard time with the management, chances are you will, too. What you do matters less than the people you work with. Picture yourself waking up in the morning. Would you be excited to go to this job? Indifferent? Would you rather starve than go back to the office? Choose a job that won't cause you psychological pain or therapy bills that could end up negating your big salary.

•• Going Out With The Boss ••

Going out for business differs from going out with your friends in many ways. One is that you can't just order a cheap beer or fruit punch, unless your boss does first — you want to look more sophisticated than that. Although you may feel stressed about being out with your boss or other important people (say, at a business luncheon), consider skipping the alcohol. This will help you stay your sharpest and avoid the hassle of which drinks are acceptable and which are not. It is just as classy to drink sparkling water with a twist of lemon or lime as to drink alcohol.

If you want to order an alcoholic drink at an evening event, it is safe and acceptable to ask for a glass of wine. Use your judgment — if it is a casual night out with people from the office, get whatever you want. If you are having brunch with your boss, be mindful of the signals you send. At brunch or lunch, it is common to order a Bloody Mary or a mimosa. If you want to look like you are having a hard drink without the effects, try a Virgin Mary (no one but you and the bartender will know that there's no vodka).

Vocabulary they didn't teach you:
"On the rocks" means with ice.
"Neat" means plain, as in a glass of whisky with no water or ice.
"Straight up" is usually used for martinis and means no ice.
"With a twist" means with a slice of lemon.

TAKING CARE OF BUSINESS

MANAGING TIME
•• Getting It All Done ••

Are you ridiculously efficient? Do you finish all your work before everyone else and then go to the beach? If so, skip this section in the interest of not wasting time.

Okay, I bet no one skipped, because:

A) most people wish there were more time in the day, and

B) the people who *do* have time left over rarely use it to relax — that's part of the reason they get so much done.

> *"The best way to get things done is to just do them."*
> — Stephanie, 45, consultant

Make a list of all the things you need and want to do. Big things, small things, work things, play things, everything.

Plan your schedule for the next day, week, and month. Write down major deadlines, then set realistic goals for the big stuff. Break each big thing into smaller, more manageable parts, and mark intermediate deadlines on the calendar as well.

Just pick something. Now that you know what you need to do, you have lots of choices about how to get it all done. This is the step that gets most people — they see so many possibilities that they don't do anything. The secret is to keep moving.

If you feel constrained by formulas, pick the task that seems most appealing and use it as a warm-up. When you're done, cross it off the list, feel the momentum you've created, and roll with it. In order to tackle the next thing, set an amount of time (say an hour and a half). Remove distractions such as your cell phone or music, and then work for the whole hour and a half. If you do this successfully, take a break. Get a snack. Walk around. Then pick something else. Just keep going.

If you need a formula, draw a square with four quadrants. Label them A, B, C, and D. In the A quadrant, write down all priorities that must be done immediately (a work deadline in two hours). In the B quadrant, list jobs that are not priorities but need to be done immediately (washing your clothes when you have no more clean socks). In the C quadrant, list tasks that are not immediately due (a grant application that needs to be turned in for review by the first of next month). In the D quadrant, list everything else — low priority, no time pressure, but you'd like to do anyway (weeding the garden). Start at A and work your way through the quadrants alphabetically.

The secret is to set small, specific goals and work through each one until it is finished. Take short breaks and recharge once you've met a goal.

Be realistic. If you set realistic goals, you will meet them. This will feel good, and you will be more likely to keep going. If you set unrealistic goals, you will get off schedule, and your schedule will fall apart. Set goals you can meet, and then reward yourself.

Find a method that works for you. Some people have a white board in their kitchen for notes, phone messages, a to-do list, and a calendar. Some carry a personal digital organizer. Others prefer a little notebook and a pen. Use whatever method works for you.

Multitasking. Can you consolidate a few activities into one? For example, I often talk to friends or family on the phone while I'm cooking dinner or eating breakfast. This lets me touch base with the people I love, and still have time to get other things done later. Other activities to combine are reading and exercising. If you have access to a stationary bike or stair machine, you can catch up on the news, study for a test, or review a document while getting in shape. Also, some studies suggest that you read faster when you have more blood flow to the brain, which happens when you are standing or when your heart is beating faster.

If you're in a real bind, you can use a little caffeine. Don't do this too often or you'll develop a tolerance and need it just to function normally. Also, too much caffeine isn't great for your health. I hate staying up late to finish important work, but the reality is, it happens, and a cola or cup of coffee can help get you through it.

•• Getting Enough Sleep ••

One key way to get sleep is to realize that you need it, and then to make it the priority. Sure, you have a lot that you *have* to do, but you'd be surprised at how much you time you waste every day that could be better spent sleeping. If you are making a presentation or taking any kind of exam, make sure to get good sleep the two nights before.

To create some extra time in the day, turn off your phone. Listen to your messages twice a day, and only return essential calls (your landlord threatening to evict you counts, your best friend wanting to chat does not). Limit the number of times you check your e-mail to three times a day (morning, midday, evening).

To make sure you get the sleep, think about when you need to wake up and plan to go to bed eight hours before that. Swear off television and personal phone calls — a short chat can turn into a marathon gabfest if you're not careful. Work hard during the day, and then at bedtime, brush up and go to sleep. This may sound overly simplified, but the reality is that you just have to do it.

MANAGING MONEY
•• Budgeting ••

Look at your lifestyle from a financial point of view. Write down how much money you have and how much you plan to make each week or month this year. (By "plan to make," I mean realistically — no planning on making millions if you work behind the counter at a fast-food chain.) Then write down all your regular expenses.

How much do you spend on groceries each week? If you don't know, keep receipts for a month and put them in a box or a notebook with sections for food, clothing, and whatever categories work for you. Tape the receipts on blank three-hole-punched pages. Do you belong to a gym with a monthly fee? How much do you spend on gas or public transportation? Account for big things (like rent), but keep track of little things, too (like the cup of coffee you buy every morning on the way to work). Get a realistic picture of how much you make compared to how much you spend.

If you make more than you spend, skip to the next section on investing. If you spend more than you make, think about how to turn this situation around: could you make a cup of coffee and take it in a travel mug instead of buying it? Could you carpool with a friend to work and split the cost of gas? Think about the little things that add up and decide what could go. A lot of young adults spend money in bars on the weekends where drinks can be really expensive. If you spend $10 every weekend partying, that's $520 a year. If you spend $20, that's $1,040 each year! Have a glass of water before you order anything. This will fill you up a little and still let you still hang out with friends.

One of the worst things you can do is to incur debt, so figure out how to make more than you are spending. Or spend less.

•• Investing ••

If you can plan well enough to end up with extra money each month, you'll thank yourself later. The earlier you start investing, the more you'll end up with later. Take a small percentage out of your earnings each month and put that money away.

A savings account is a simple place to start managing your money. It's more accessible than an IRA or a mutual fund since you can take money out of it without a penalty or brokerage fee, but it will give you significantly less interest.

An individual retirement account (IRA) is a good place to start saving if you won't need access to the money anytime soon. This type of account lets you save money before taxes and allows considerable flexibility in terms of where the money is invested. The catch is that if you want to withdraw the money before you retire (or at age 59½), you will have to pay a penalty (usually 10%). Many employers offer to automatically deduct money from your paycheck to be placed in an IRA, and it is a good idea to contribute to the fund monthly. There are five types of IRAs: Traditional, Education, Simplified Employee Pension (SEP), Simple, and Roth. Each type has advantages and different rules about putting money in and taking money out. Look around online or talk to your bank or investment firm about which type is best for you. If you are young and have time before you retire, go for the most aggressive investing option. In the long run, your money will grow most here. If you are older, choose a more conservative IRA plan.

> *"I put fifty dollars a month (pre-tax) into my IRA. That's less than the government takes, and since I'm young, I know it will turn into a lot more later."*
> — Will, 22, paralegal

Mutual funds allow you to give your money to a firm that will pool it with other people's money, invest in a number of stocks, and thus cut losses. You can choose whichever type of mutual fund pleases you. Some only invest in foreign companies or tech companies or socially-conscious companies or broad general interests, to name a few.

The stock market. If you have more time and want to play the game solo, you can invest in the stock market. In general, you need a broker, whether a real person or an online brokerage site. There is usually a fee for each trade or a monthly fee. Choose stocks in companies that you know and like. Research before investing. How has this company done in the past? What does it do that is useful? Will this service or product still be useful tomorrow and in a year? Once you have decided what stock to buy, watch it for a few weeks. See the highs and lows, and then put in an order to buy near the low. For example, if a stock oscillates between twelve and fourteen dollars a share for two weeks, put in the order to buy at twelve. Although this may not happen immediately, chances are that it will hit that low sometime over the course of the next week. Watch your investments and stay up to date with your investment companies.

A dirty little secret: don't try to "pick" stocks. Not even the best brokers can outwit the market. A good illustration of this comes from a well-respected publication in the industry that lists how the predictions of top analysts fair versus the predictions of a dartboard, which picks stocks randomly. The dartboard almost always wins. So, you might want to consider investing in an index fund, which tracks the performance of the market, which tends to rise over the long term. Keep in mind that any time you play with the stock market you are taking on risk, but if you have the time and some money, it can pay off.

Regardless of how you choose to invest, shop around. Different banks and investment companies will give you different deals, so it pays to be an informed consumer.

•• Digging Yourself Out of a Hole ••

Many younger adults get into debt using credit cards. It can feel like you have a lot more money than you have, and it is harder to keep track of purchases when you don't need to actually hand over any cash. Credit cards are convenient to carry, but you should follow a few simple rules to avoid debt:

✔ Never buy something with a credit card that costs more than what you have in your checking account.

✓ Pay your bill in full each month. If you don't pay it off, the remaining balance begins to accrue interest. This money can add up, and the small things you buy can end up costing much more than their original price tags.

✓ If you get into debt, stop using cards all together — cut them up if you have to. Stick to a strict budget, and pay off more than the minimum amount due each month. If you don't acquire new debt, you'll be able to work off the old one. Also, consider transferring the balance of your credit card to a lower-interest card. Many credit-card companies offer low or zero percent introductory rates that buy you a little more time before your debt starts multiplying. Still, even if you get one of these deals, stop spending until you pay off the old debt.

Good debt vs. bad debt. Good debt is low-interest debt with no monthly fees. An example of this is student loan debt. Good debt, however, is only good if you make regular payments and use the flexibility it provides to make more money than you are losing through interest paid (i.e., do not use student loans to go buy yourself presents — like all debt, you do have to pay the money back). On average, the stock market makes about twelve to thirteen percent yearly, whereas your student loans accrue interest at about three to five percent. If you invest wisely, you can make money on the difference. However, if you spend the money, you will just end up with a big amount to pay off at the end of your loan period.

Bad debt is debt that has a high interest rate or requires a monthly fee. Examples include credit-card debt and the financing on that new stereo you've had your eye on.

•• Balancing Your Checkbook ••

Debit cards and credit cards make it even harder to think about "balancing a checkbook," seeing as how most people don't write many checks anymore. Yet, it's still important to know how much money you're spending versus how much you're making. Go over your bank statement each month to check it against receipts — banks make mistakes sometimes, too. To balance your checkbook, keep track of each check as you write it. Record who got the check, the check number, how much you spent, and what it was for. At the end of the month, add up the total and check it against your bank statement. Some people write down their starting balance at the beginning of each month and then subtract from it each time they write a check so that they always know how much is in their account. This helps avoid bouncing checks.

One way to stop spending more than you have is to use only cash in stores, and to limit yourself to a certain amount of cash per week. This will force you to pay attention to how much you spend and to stop when you run out.

•• Contracts ••

As you move into situations in the "real world" and the sums of money you are dealing with increase, it is very important to understand and keep track of the contracts you enter into. A contract is an agreement in which one party makes an offer and another party accepts the offer in exchange for something else. For example, if you offer to sell me your car for $75 and I agree, that is a verbal contract. If, on the other hand, I say I'll give you $75 for nothing, that is not a contract. In the first case, I am obliged to pay you the money if you give me the car. In the second case, however, I don't have to pay you anything, since you are not giving me anything in exchange.

When you enter into any verbal or written contract, such as an apartment lease, an agreement to purchase a car, or a work-for-hire arrangement, make sure that you understand exactly what you will be expected to do, what you will receive in exchange, and all of the smaller details. For example, if you agree to paint your neighbor's house to earn some extra cash, you should agree, in writing, on how much you will charge for your labor, who will pay for supplies, when you will get paid, etc. If you don't write out all the details, your neighbor may expect you to pay for supplies as part of the labor cost or you may expect to get paid weekly while he or she expects to pay you upon completion of the job. If you write out the agreement in advance, both parties know what to expect from one another. And you will be able to plan for when you will have the money. This makes it easier to budget and to set aside some money for a rainy day (see page 74 on budgeting).

> *"I sold my car for $300 to a guy who worked in the cafeteria here. He didn't have the money right when I was selling but I told him it was no problem since I see him every day. I told him he could give it to me when he had it. Then, a few days after I gave him the car, he got fired and I never saw him again. If I had had proof of our contract in writing, I could have taken it to small claims court and gotten my $300."*
> — Douglas, 31, history teacher and lawyer

You should keep copies of all contracts and any other paperwork involved to refer back to and to have as proof in case the person or business you are contracting with defaults on the agreement. Receipts for products you have purchased can also provide good proof of contract; they can be very useful if you end up with a faulty product. A little known fact is that even if a company provides a disclaimer that says, for example, "the pencil you bought will not necessarily write on paper," you still have the right to expect it to carry out its basic function. You have the right to return it if it doesn't, in this case, write on paper. Returning it will be much easier if you've kept your receipt.

EDUCATION
•• Scholarships and Grants ••

Depending on your age, race, and family income level, you may be eligible for various forms of financial aid. Your university will probably help you figure out the standard federal and university scholarships, but there are many other types of grants. Often, individual towns or religious institutions put aside money to help students from the community. Writing an essay or two can land you major cash. Search the Internet or look around in a bookstore to find organizations that give money for academic pursuits. Some grants help with tuition, and others give money for a new computer or for transportation to and from school, etc.

If you've graduated from an undergraduate program, look into scholarships and grants to help you pursue graduate work or independent projects. Rhodes, Fulbright, and Marshall scholarships are some of the really competitive ones, but many colleges offer their own internal grants, so ask a dean or academic adviser if your school offers this type of grant.

When applying for any type of scholarship or grant:

✔ Proposals and essays should show who you are and demonstrate something unique that you have accomplished or hope to accomplish. Don't just say what you think they want to hear. Tell them about yourself, giving specific evidence of why you are the best person for the scholarship or grant.

✔ Give yourself plenty of time. Reread your application, then show it to as many other people as you can (parents, old professors, friends) to get feedback.

•• Alternative Sources of Funding ••

The U.S. Armed Forces offer educational grants for study after serving — check out the new Montgomery GI Bill or the Navy College Fund, for example. The armed forces also offer the opportunity to earn college credits while serving and help paying off student loans.

Also, many employers will pay for some graduate study. If you're considering getting a higher degree but don't have the money at the moment, look for a job with a company that has a policy of funding employee education. Companies often pay for tuition, books, and even transportation.

COMPUTERS
•• Avoid Losing Time With Lost Files ••

Always back up your work. If you religiously back up your documents, both on your hard drive and somewhere else, you will not fall victim to the common but horrible situation in which you have spent huge amounts of time on an important document and then lose everything when the system crashes.

If you didn't remember to do the above, you may still be okay. Most word-processing programs save automatically once every ten to thirty minutes. If you have an older computer that freezes a lot, change this setting so your computer automatically saves every five minutes. If your document has been automatically saved, when you reopen the program, it will either notify you that it has recovered the document, or you will find a recovered version in your documents or temp folder. To discover out where such a file might be stored if you can't find it right away, open a new document and try to save it. Note where the computer wants to put the file, and then check for your old file there.

If you lose a file or encounter another major problem that you don't know how to fix, there are several places you might look for help. If you're in school, check if your institution provides tech support. Many companies and businesses also have tech support. The help center will know places to look that you might not have tried. If you aren't in school or employed, call a friend who knows a decent amount about computers. You can also search for chat rooms and newsgroups devoted to computer advice or type the name of the program or hardware that is giving you trouble into a search engine.

•• When Programs Crash or the Machine Runs Slowly ••

If your programs crash often, restart, restart, restart! Many problems associated with computers can be eased by restarting the machine periodically. You can also reformat the hard drive and reinstall your operating system. However this should only be used as a last resort. You should make sure to back up *everything* you might want in the future on separate disks before doing this: reformatting erases everything on your computer and lets you start fresh. This often fixes problems, but, again, make sure everything is backed up before you start.

If your computer is running slowly, you may need more Random Access Memory (RAM). RAM for desktop computers is cheap and can be easily ordered online or bought at any electronics store. If you are unsure how much RAM your computer can take, opt for the store option even though buying online will be cheaper. A sales representative can tell you what type of RAM to buy and how much you'll need to fix your problem. You may want to let them install it for you, although it is relatively simple to do it yourself. To install the RAM, you will need to remove the computer case, consult your manual to find out where the RAM goes, and slide it in. If you do not feel comfortable doing this yourself but the electronics store wants to charge you an arm and a leg, keep in mind that it is a very simple procedure. If you know anyone who knows a little about the insides of computers, they can likely help you.

•• Things to Consider When Buying a Computer ••

What will I be using my new computer for?

If you just want to do word processing, you can get away with a much cheaper, simpler machine than you can if you want to edit your own movies. Computers are good enough now that anything being sold will be more than adequate for word processing, sending e-mails, and surfing the web.

Laptop vs. desktop?

In general you pay more for small size. Therefore a laptop computer will cost more than its equivalent desktop computer. Laptops are also more difficult to upgrade and are easily stolen. You should consider a laptop if you travel a lot or want to work in several different locations, but consider a desktop if you do most of your work at home and are concerned about price.

New vs. used?

Like buying a new car, buying a new computer means you're getting a machine that doesn't already have problems. While it may be cheaper to buy a used or refurbished computer, it may not be compatible with your software. Some programs, such as brand-new photo/video editors or action games, may require a faster machine than you can buy used. If you do decide to buy a used machine, buy it from a reputable dealer who gives you some type of warranty.

Mac vs. PC?

The Mac vs. PC debate has taken on the feel of religious fanaticism. Disregard people who tell you that one is absolutely better than the other. For the same speed machine, a PC will cost less than a Mac, but Macs have certain kinds of software available for free. Macs tend to come with less RAM, but often have nicer processors. It really comes down to personal preference. I'd say compare individual machines — not brand names.

•• Parts ••

When buying a new computer, you should know what you're getting inside. The following is a list of major components and what they are good for:

The central processing unit (CPU). With a fast CPU (processor) your applications will open faster. Anything that you start running and leave for a while will be done sooner with a fast CPU (i.e., if you wanted to copy music to your computer by encoding songs on a CD as MP3 files, that would be faster with a fast CPU). If you buy a cheap computer, the processor may list the same "speed" as a more expensive one, but will feel slower because it has less temporary storage in it (called cache). Although it is expensive to get more cache, it makes a big difference in terms of how fast the machine feels.

Random-access memory (RAM). As mentioned above, RAM is temporary storage. When you start a program, it uses RAM. When you stop the program, the RAM is freed. The more RAM you have available for programs to use, the smoother your computer will feel. If you want to run several programs at once, or if you want things to open, close, and operate more crisply, you need more RAM. Large programs now require a lot of RAM by themselves. RAM is relatively cheap to upgrade, so go for a little more than suggested.

Hard drive. Your hard drive is permanent storage space. You won't fill any standard hard drive with text documents, but consider more space if you plan to store music, movies, or really high-quality pictures on your computer. About 175 songs or one hour of video equals one gigabyte (GB).

Other things to look for in a hard drive are seek time, buffer size, and RPM. These measures determine how fast you can get information to and from the drive. Ideally you want a lower seek time, a higher RPM, and a larger buffer.

Video card. Standard video cards are totally adequate for most applications. Think about spending more to get a better video card if you plan to play a lot of action games, or if you plan to use your computer as a DVD player by hooking it up to your television.

•• Unwanted Junk Mail ••

Do you get ridiculous amounts of e-mail from companies you've never heard of trying to sell you stuff? Join the club. This type of e-mail is called "spam," and although it is a pain to deal with, it can be avoided and reduced by taking some precautions.

✔ Never give out your preferred e-mail address to anyone but your friends, family, and people who must contact you for business. Avoid spam before it happens.

✔ Open a new "junk" account — there are many free e-mail accounts available for this, such as Hotmail and Yahoo. Give out your new address every time you want to buy something online, sign up for a mailing list, or subscribe to a service. Many companies trade mailing lists and sell your information to other companies who, in turn, do the same. Pretty soon, your information has traveled far and wide and you are the recipient of tons of junk e-mail. Using a separate account for transactions that are likely to put you on these lists will reduce the daily load of spam in your regular account.

✔ Don't send forwards to your whole contact list. Doing so adds your name to the list, and this information could find its way into the hands of a spammer. Also, forwards are almost always really stupid and I, personally, hate receiving them.

✔ Most e-mail programs have a filter system that allows you to specify the types of e-mails you will accept (i.e., you can refuse all e-mails addressed to more than one person, if you like, or you can refuse all e-mails with specific words in the subject line). If your e-mail program doesn't have this feature, you can buy spam-killing programs. They are usually just simple filters, but it's better than nothing.

Transportation

BUYING A CAR
•• Before You Begin ••

Ask yourself the following questions:

✔ What will I use this car for? Do I need a big van for carting stuff to and from college, or a compact car that will get good mileage on my commute to work? Do I want to save money (and the environment) by buying a hybrid gas/electric car?

✔ Do I want an automatic or a manual transmission?

✔ Which features are important to me?

Give yourself plenty of time to talk to lots of dealers (or look through lots of want ads). If you're buying a new car (you lucky duck), read reviews, check safety ratings, and then call each dealer to ask for a bid. Tell them you're shopping around, and make notes about the managers who seem trustworthy and who give you the lowest prices.

•• New or Used? ••

Do you want a new or used car? This question often translates to, "How much money do you have?" Keep in mind that new cars lose value quickly.

If you're buying used, your first question will be, "Should I buy from an individual or from a dealership?" The pros to buying from someone you know are that you know what kind of treatment the car has had and, chances are, they won't try to pull a fast one on you. The pros to buying at a dealership are that you will probably get some kind of warranty and dealers tend to keep careful records on each car.

> **Another option:** Buy from your mechanic. If you don't have a car, you probably don't have a mechanic you trust, but maybe your parents or friends do. You can usually get a lower price than at a dealership, and you have more of a guarantee than if you bought from a want ad.

•• The Process ••

Before you buy, find out about:

- ✔ Mileage and how the car has been driven. Freeway driving is easier on the car than city driving.

- ✔ Why the car is for sale. Does it have specific problems?

- ✔ How many owners the car has had. If it has gone through three in the past year, this may indicate a major, ongoing problem.

Pay attention to these answers, and the way they are given. If someone rushes through a muffled explanation of why they want to get rid of this "amazingly wonderful" car or hesitates when you ask if it has problems, think twice. If in doubt, walk away.

After obtaining information about your potential new rides, go for test drives in your favorites. If possible:

✔ Take a friend or relative with you, preferably someone who knows a little bit about cars or has a great sense of style.

✔ Test it on a highway and on a small street.

✔ Hold the wheel loosely and pay attention to the alignment. Does the car veer one way or the other?

✔ Test out all of the features you might want to use (the stereo, A/C, heating, wipers, blinkers, etc.).

✔ Make sure all of the seat belts work.

✔ Check out the trunk, the upholstery, and the body. If there are portions of the paint job that don't match, the car was probably repaired after a crash. You can check the paint to see if the car may have been in an accident by opening the hood or trunk and feeling the inside edge where the body folds from the outside to the inside of the trunk or engine compartment. If you can feel a ridge where the masking tape may have been, the car has been painted. You may want to walk away. Also, you can use CARFAX®, a service that tells you a car's ownership history and whether it has been in an accident.

Once you're satisfied that you've found the right car, take it to a technician.

✔ Get a pre-buying inspection, and make sure the mechanic notes, in writing, any defects.

✔ Get a written estimate of how much it would cost to put the car in tip-top shape.

✔ Ask the seller to do the repairs or to deduct the estimate from the car's price.

> *"When I bought my first car, I was so nervous that I would miss some really obvious detail and the car would fall apart on the way home. A friend suggested that I show the car to my mechanic before buying. I was like, 'Wow, you can do that? I'd be so offended if I were selling the car.' Apparently that's totally normal, though. My car passed with flying colors and I'm really happy with it. If someone won't let you do it, it's because they've got something to hide."*
> — Angelina, 28, programmer

Don't be afraid to bargain — you are about to shell out a hefty amount of cash, and many people advertise prices that take negotiation into account. Dealers usually build in a profit margin that can amount to several thousand dollars for a used car. They are entitled to make a profit, but the savvy consumer will attempt to bargain.

•• The Paperwork ••

Finally, if the car has passed your inspection as well as the technician's, make sure that all the papers are in order. You should get the title (depending on your state) and registration, the owner's manual, a bill of sale (with the date, the names and addresses of the contracting parties, the year, make, and model of the car, and the vehicle ID number), a warranty, repair documentation, and the smog or emissions certificate.

Once you're finally ready to buy, shop around for the best financing. Keep in mind that a bank may give you better loan rates than a dealership, but this is not always the case. Get a quote from your bank, take it with you to the dealer, and find out if they can beat it. If you have good credit, the dealership might just come through. Once you have the financing in order, fork over the cash, then drive off into the sunset.

•• Leasing ••

If you don't want to buy a car, consider leasing. You can get a new car with a warranty, but you don't have to pay the full price of a new car. Leasing can end up being expensive, though, if you go over your allowed mileage or cause major damage to the car. If you lease, make sure you get gap insurance. This covers you if something bad (such as theft) happens to your car before the lease ends, so you won't be held responsible for paying for something you can no longer use.

•• If Cars Are Too Expensive... ••

Consider paying for gas in exchange for rides. You can offer to chip in on gas if you know a colleague who lives close to you and might be able to give you rides to and from work.

Public transportation can often get you to your destination quickly and inexpensively. Plus it's better for the environment and will probably give you a chance to walk outside for a few minutes, too.

Biking is great exercise and can be as fast as driving (fewer traffic concerns, no worries about parking). Biking cuts down on pollution and will keep you in shape. People at the office will admire your toughness as well as your hot new bod.

TAKING CARE OF YOUR CAR
•• Fixing a Flat Tire ••

It's a good idea to go practice this procedure in your driveway with someone who knows what he or she is doing, so you're not left hitchhiking if you break down. Always keep a spare tire in your trunk as well as a jack and a lug wrench. This is almost always included in a new car, but check to make sure before you run into trouble. You may also want to keep a copy of this book handy for instructions.

✔ Step one: After finding the jack, look for a big piece of metal that's part of the car's frame to support the jack. Don't put the jack under the bumper since this will likely break under the weight. Also avoid the area right next to the tire since the car's suspension will absorb a lot of your energy trying to jack it up. A good place can usually be found just in front of the tire.

✔ Step two: Use the jack to lift up your car. Make sure the jack stays solidly under the car and flat on the ground. After jacking the car up slightly, before the wheel is off the ground, it's a good idea to loosen the lug nuts. Don't take them all the way off; just break the seal. If you wait until the tire is off the ground, pushing on the wrench will cause the tire to spin, making it tough to remove the nuts. After they are loose, jack the car up so the tire is above the ground.

✔ Step three: Unscrew the old tire and pull it off. A lot of cars have hubcaps, and a lot of hubcaps have fake screws on them. If this is the case with your car, pull the hubcap off (a screwdriver helps to pry it off) and the real screws should be underneath. Your jack will have some type of wrench associated with it to fit the tire's screws.

✔ Step four: Ease the new tire on and screw it into place.

✔ Step five: Lower jack so tire rests on the ground and tighten screws. Replace hubcap.

✔ Step six: Remove the jack by hitting the release or screwing back down. If your spare tire is significantly smaller than your other tires, that's okay, but you should replace it with a full-size tire as soon as possible.

•• Tire Pressure ••

Monitoring your tire pressure will help you get better mileage and extend the life of your tires. Look at your tires. If they look a little bulgy, the pressure is probably too low. To check the tire pressure, use a pressure gauge (it looks like a pen and has a little piece of plastic that comes in and out of the end with a satisfying clicky noise). Unscrew the air valve and hook on your gauge. Often the appropriate pressure will be printed on the tire, inside the driver's side door, or inside the gas cap. If it isn't there, check your owner's manual. Normal pressures are in the high twenties or low thirties. If your pressure is higher than the listed pressure and it's hot out, don't worry, that's normal. If it's significantly lower, go to a gas station and use the free air provided there.

•• Oil ••

Check your oil level regularly. Open the hood. There will be a big cap that says "Oil." That's not what you want. Look for a dipstick that you don't have to unscrew, which will probably say, "Check oil." Pull it out and wipe it off with a rag or paper towel. Put it back in. Pull it out again and note the level where the liquid rose on the stick. The stick will have a cross-hatched area. You want the oil to be somewhere in that range. If it's below the recommended level, buy a container of oil at a gas station and pour it in the hole covered by the cap that says "Oil" — not where you checked the dipstick. Have your oil changed by a mechanic every 5,000 miles.

•• Coolant ••

You also need to monitor your coolant level. Under the hood you will find a clear plastic tub with green liquid inside. There will be a line called the cold fill line. The level of the green coolant should be around that line when the engine's cold and slightly below it if the engine is running.

•• Things to Keep in the Car ••

Just in case, you should always keep your trunk stocked with:

A blanket, in case you break down in the cold.

Your car jack, wrench, and spare tire, unless the jack has its own place under the hood.

A copy of this book, in case you need instructions about how to change a tire, check your oil, etc.

Jumper cables, in case you leave the lights on by mistake or need to play a really long game of pickup basketball and must use your car's headlights to light the court (not recommended).

Reflective triangles (or flares), in case you break down at night.

A first-aid kit, for boo-boos and more serious things.

Basic tools, if you know how to use them or have passengers who might.

A flashlight, for telling scary stories when you break down at night (you know how cool your face looks when lit from below), and for more practical things. Have some spare batteries, too.

A brightly-colored (or white) cloth, to flag down help in a bind.

Other things to keep in the car (usually in the glove compartment):
— Your insurance and registration info
— Some money (just in case)
— A pen and paper
— A cell phone and charger (in case of emergencies)
— Regional and local maps

Relationships

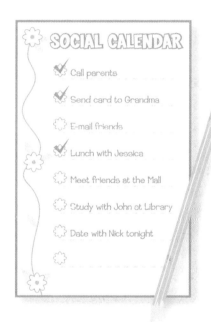

FAMILY
•• Talking to Your Parents ••

You miss your parents, but you end up fighting every time you talk to them. This is a common phenomenon. You are stressed about work. They are stressed about home repairs (or visa versa). You call to say hello, or to ask for a loan for your home repairs. Everything is going well until (fill in the blank: they want you to come visit more and you're too busy, or they ask about your job that doesn't pay enough money, or you're rushing out the door and don't have time to talk).

You could get an unlisted number, but the easiest way to keep your cool is to think about what tends to frustrate you, and to plan ahead. For example:

- ✔ If you can't stand telling the same story twice (once to your stepdad, and then again to your mom), ask them both to pick up a phone before you start talking.

- ✔ If you know they want to see more of you, but you can't go home often, figure out when you will be there and mention it before they get a chance to ask. "I'm really excited to see you for Thanksgiving. I need to work hard until then, but it'll be great to relax together." This lets them know you're not avoiding them, reassures them that you love them, and gives them something to look forward to.

- ✔ If you know they don't approve of your job, or boyfriend, or lifestyle, ask questions about what they've been up to — believe it or not, they have lives, too. This will allow you to have a conversation without dealing with heavy subjects. My advice: deal with heavy stuff in person. It's much harder to fix wounds long distance. You get the point. Keep in mind that they love you. Take deep breaths. You are independent now and that might be hard for them to take, but in the long run touching base over the phone helps.

•• Impressing Other People's Parents ••

If you want to impress your significant other's parents when invited to dinner in their home, you should:

✔ Bring a small gift or a bottle of wine. This indicates that you appreciate their invitation and want to give something back.

✔ If dinner is still in the works when you arrive, offer to help. Asking what you can do shows that you care. They may tell you to relax or they may give you a job to do. If given a job, do it with a smile.

✔ Offer to set the table. In case you don't know the "right" way to do this, see the diagram below.

✔ At dinner, remember the basic manners you learned as a kid: wait until everyone has food and is seated to begin eating, don't talk with your mouth full, keep your elbows off the table, and put your napkin on your lap.

✔ When someone asks you to pass them something (i.e., the salt), it is rude to use it before giving it to them.

✔ You can eat some things with your fingers (pizza, bread, tacos, asparagus if it is without sauce or dressing, corn on the cob, cookies, fruit, less formal food like burgers, and fries, etc.) but for greasy food or fancy food, use your utensils.

✔ In the U.S., you're supposed to fork everything (even hard to handle items like peas and cherry tomatoes) but in Europe, it's fine to use bread or a knife to help secure these types of food, and I think you can get by with it in the U.S. as well.

✔ Help clear the table when everyone is finished. This extra effort will earn you major bonus points.

✔ In general, take your cues from the hosts. If they are comfortable with their elbows on the table during discussion and you are uncomfortable with your hands in your lap, it's probably okay to do what they do.

FRIENDS
•• Staying in Touch ••

People like to know that you're thinking about them. A quick phone call to say hello or a real, paper letter will often make someone's day. If, however, you are not the mushy type or just don't have time for long letters, you can still stay in touch. Here are some easy ways to do so.

- ✓ Reference a conversation that you had with someone about them: "I was talking to my mom yesterday and she asked how you were. I realized I haven't heard from you in a while, and so I wanted to see what's up."

- ✓ Send an article that they might be interested in: "I saw this in the *Daily Batton,* and thought about your love of kangaroos. I never knew there was so much to know about the life cycle of marsupials!" This works for cutouts from the daily paper and for online references — most online journals will allow you to bookmark a page to send to a friend. Include a short, personal note along with the reference — "I'm still working at Rabbit's Foot Press, and the new house is great. I'd love to hear your news, too!" This is fast, easy, and lets the person know you are thinking of them.

- ✓ Send a postcard. This limits the amount you need to write and can be funny (if you're not on vacation) or easy (if you *are* on vacation and have the time). A postcard is a low-pressure device to tell someone that you like him or her. An alternative is to make or buy a ridiculous greeting card ("Happy 80th Birthday" for your twenty-five-year-old friend). Humor is a good way to stay in touch, while not seeming too demanding.

These techniques work for your family as well. An e-mail to Aunt Genie or a postcard to Grandma will help you stay connected and make her day.

•• Making New Friends in a Strange Place ••

Moving can be stressful for many reasons, but one of the biggest is leaving your old community. It's easiest to make new acquaintances right as you move in since this will give you a good excuse to be outgoing. Even if you've lived in your neighborhood for a little while, there are many places to make new friends.

As you move in, knock on the neighbors' doors and introduce yourself. Consider having a potluck dinner at your house. Ask everyone to bring a little food, and that way you can meet the people on your block. This will also show them how friendly you are and that you want to be friends.

Join a sports league. You don't have to be good at the sport — most leagues are just for fun. Team membership is a good bonding experience. If you find that you like one or two people in particular, ask them if they want to grab dinner after the game. This will give you a chance to get to know them better. Asking more than one person, or the whole team, will make it seem less intimidating and will take some of the conversation pressure off once you're there.

Volunteer for a community organization or at a local park. Teach English as a second language one afternoon a week or plant trees at the local senior home. You will meet other volunteers and people within your community. Volunteering also can be a fun way to make your community a better place.

Organize cheap outings and invite new friends. Are there local spots associated with legends of the past? Does your town have a museum? How about a park? Pretend you are a tourist in your own town and try to see the place with new eyes. If that doesn't strike your fancy, get in the car and go to a nearby town or city that you don't visit often and check out what they have to offer.

ROMANCE
•• Asking Someone Out ••

Oh my gosh! The hottest girl just walked by. How can I secure some time with her, without seeming too anxious?

Straightforward. "Would you like to have coffee with me?" Or if you're especially confident: "I think you're attractive." This is best if she has been eyeing you, you're confident that you don't have any weird stain on your shirt, and you haven't done anything worth gossiping about recently. It actually works.

Ask for advice. If you're at the grocery store in the pet food aisle, ask if she has a dog. Tell her a little about your pet and ask if her pet might like to have a play date with your pet... If you're in the cereal aisle, ask if she's tried the generic version of your favorite cereal — "Is it as good as the real thing?" If you're at a party, ask if she knows where the host keeps glasses or more chips or whatever. Smile, and you've made contact.

The small gift. "I have all of these daisies/bouncy balls/cans of soda/whatever that a friend just gave me. Do you want one?"

No plan. "Hi, my name's Alex. What's yours?" This is good if she looks friendly (and if your name is Alex). Hey, you've got nothing to lose. Remember to smile.

Things in common. She's wearing a T-shirt advertising a band you like or an organization you support. "Hey, did you see the Bungaree's last concert? I heard it was (awesome/worse than usual/whatever you heard)." This works best if it is genuine. It also works if she has a cool toy on her key chain: "Hey, do you know how to solve that Rubik's cube? Let me give you a hand." Don't fake interests because you'll look stupid, and eventually if things work out, she'll find out that you were lying (which is very unattractive).

When asking someone out, it's best to avoid:

The fake bump. You know, where you pretend to trip and fall on her — too risky since it will probably look fake, and will certainly make you look uncoordinated.

The bad pick up line. "Hey baby, are those space pants..." No.

Pity. "I just got out of a long relationship, and I need you to make it better..." Not good.

•• Polite Rejection ••

The grossest guy just asked me out. How can I ditch the invitation without seeming like a total jerk, hurting his feelings, or leading him on?

The one-time invite. "Do you want to get a drink with me tonight?" If you feel comfortable being blunt, that may be the best plan: "No, but thanks!" Smile to show you appreciate the offer and to put the asker at ease.

If you don't feel comfortable being this straightforward, say you have other plans: "Sorry, I'm busy, but thanks for the offer."

Don't get into an elaborate story about what the plans are, since elaborate lies lead to trouble later. Avoid the phrase "maybe some other time" if you have no intention of ever going out with this person. If he presses you about an alternate time ("Well, how about next Tuesday?"), make it clear (gently) that you won't be free any time soon: "I don't have a lot of time in my life for that right now," or a simple "Thanks a lot for the offer, but I can't really accept." This will let him know to move on.

The friend who wants more. "Can I kiss you?" or "We've been friends so long, I was wondering if maybe you want more?" Presumably you care about this person and want to stay friends with him. If this is true, keep in mind that telling you how he feels might have felt like a big risk to him, so be careful with your response (no laughing and asking "Did you really think that was a possibility?!") Tell the truth. If you feel flattered, say so. Say something to affirm that you value his friendship, "You are such an important person in my life." Then make it clear that you value the relationship too much to jeopardize it with a kiss. If you mean it, say you want to stay friends and you know that even one kiss would sabotage that. Assume that everything is fine; act like your relationship hasn't changed and this awkward moment never happened. If your friend is acting weird, have another conversation in which you explain that you still aren't interested but don't want to lose his friendship: "I was really flattered, but that's just not what I want from this relationship." Understand that it may be hard for him to spend time with you right away since he might feel weird or need to deal with his own feelings. Call him up once in a while to let him know you still want to be friends, and invite him to group activities. Try to understand how he is feeling and just be gentle.

Away From Home

TRAVEL
•• Cheap Transport ••

Surprisingly, sometimes flying can be the cheapest way to go. You can usually find the best deals online at sites that specialize in cheap flights, but sometimes travel agents have special fares that are not listed elsewhere (student fares or promotions). Another benefit to buying through a travel agent is that you may be able to get a more flexible ticket than you could online or directly from the airline.

For travel in Europe, many Americans opt to buy a Eurail Pass that allows them a certain number of days of travel within the European Union at a set cost. If you want to do this, you must buy the pass *before* you leave the U.S. since Eurail passes are not sold in Europe (weirdly enough). Be aware, however, that there are several *very* cheap airlines that operate in Europe and might be a lot less expensive than the train especially if you want to fly to or from London. Look around online before buying. Keep in mind that you don't necessarily need to be a student to get low fares. In Europe, anyone under twenty-six can get cheaper rates.

Making a reservation is not the same as buying a ticket. In general, the longer you wait, the more expensive tickets become. If you don't have a specific destination in mind, however, some travel sites/agencies offer cheap, last-minute deals that usually include airfare and hotel.

If you can't get the flight you want, consider going standby. For example, if you booked a ticket from New York to Chicago for 3:00 PM on November 5, but later decide it would be better arrive earlier, you might want to change your ticket. Often, however, airlines charge a large fee to change your flight. Never fear, you may still be able to get on an earlier flight. You must have a ticket for the day you want to fly, but you can try to get on an earlier flight by showing up and checking if there is space on the flight you really want. This is called going standby. You will have to wait until all the passengers with regular tickets check in, but if there is space left, it's yours. If there isn't any space, you haven't really lost out because you still have a regular ticket for later that day. If you are considering going standby, check with individual airlines to find out how far in advance you need to show up to be considered for standby and if there are any extra fees.

Get bumped, go for free next time: Another money-saving option for those of you with flexible schedules is to "get bumped." Airlines overbook certain flights banking on the fact that some people won't show up. When everyone does, however, they have a problem (not enough space on the plane). In order to fix the problem, they will ask some people to take a later flight, and in exchange will give them up to several hundred dollars in vouchers for free travel in the future. Many people either don't know about this or have somewhere they need to be. If you have the time, get to the airport a little early and check in with plenty of time before your flight. Then at the departure desk, ask if the flight is full. If it is, tell the attendant that you are willing to get bumped. They will probably be happy to take your name. To increase the chance that they will need to bump you, plan your travel far in advance and book flights at highly-traveled times. Right before and after major holidays are busy times, and so are most Friday afternoons and Sunday evenings.

•• Packing Light ••

To bring or not to bring, that is the question. When packing, it's tempting to bring *all* your favorite clothes as well as some backup stuff in case you get dirty, shoes to go with each outfit and three different sports, and your hair dryer. Stop right there. First of all, if you're traveling abroad you won't be able to plug in your dryer, and second of all, before you know it, you can barely lift your suitcase, let alone carry it from the airport.

To lighten your load, consider your destination and how long you'll be gone. You don't need that much more for a month than you do for a week. Will you be able to do laundry? If so, bring a week's worth of clothing or less. For long vacations, will you have access to a supermarket or drugstore? If so, leave the shampoo and conditioner at home. Bring a travel-sized container of any toiletry that you'll need in the first few days of your trip and then buy the rest when you get there.

Before putting anything into a suitcase, lay everything out on your bed. Eliminate half of what you thought you needed. If there are eight T-shirts on your bed, bring four. If you think you will need to dress up, bring one nice outfit. Choose something that can be accessorized in different ways — bring two ties or a few different scarves, different jewelry, or a cool hat. This also goes for shoes: bring one pair of comfortable walking shoes and one pair of dressier shoes. Choose dress shoes that you can also wear with casual clothing to maximize efficiency.

Pack underwear and socks in plastic baggies. Get all the air out before sealing them. This method compresses volume, and also allows you to easily find clean socks when you get there.

•• The Essentials ••

You should always carry the following items.

✔ Photocopies of your passport (and visa if you have one), important phone numbers, insurance information, your travel itinerary, and emergency contact information. Leave copies with someone you trust at home.

✔ Prescription medications and refills (don't count on being able to get more while away). You should also have a copy of the prescription so that you can fill it in an emergency (you ran out or lost the supply you brought). Make sure that the prescription lists the generic name as well as the brand name.

✔ Contraception. If you are sexually active and traveling outside of the U.S., bring your own contraception including condoms, since you may not have access to these products abroad or the quality may be worse.

✔ Extra plastic bags in case your stuff gets wet, and to hold dirty laundry.

Tips for getting a passport: Give yourself at least six weeks before you want to go abroad. It is possible to get a passport in under two weeks, but it involves going to a local court house, standing in line, and paying an expedite fee. If you go ahead of time, you can apply at the post office, which involves filling out some forms, giving them two passport pictures, and sending in the application (there is a fee for this as well, but it's much less than if you need it done quickly). Once you have your passport, make sure to keep it somewhere safe and protected. If you lose it while abroad, it is harder than you might think to get a new one, and you won't be able to leave the country you're in without it.

•• Pre-departure Arrangements ••

A few days before you leave, pack, go over your itinerary, and make sure that all of your insurance information is in order. When planning a trip, you may want to buy traveler's insurance. Plans vary but can cover things like missed transportation, stolen items while away, and even your health. If your current health insurance doesn't cover you while you're out of the country (or your state), it's a good idea to get travel health insurance.

You should also read about your destination. Knowing a lot before you get there will help you have a more enjoyable trip. Learning about the customs and culture of your destination can save you a lot of embarrassment. If you don't know the customs, you're likely to break them, which can offend some and just make you look silly to others. If you are a woman, this is especially important since some countries treat women differently based on the way they are dressed or how they act. It can actually be dangerous for you not to know these details.

When you're ready to leave, make sure that you have all your luggage and leave a copy of your itinerary with someone at home. Go online or call the airline/train/bus company to make sure that your transport is on schedule. This especially applies to trains because you don't need as much time at the station before departure, and they are often quite late. Be careful, though — trains can sometimes make up time, so get there a little before the projected departure time.

WHEN INVITED OUT
•• Dining in a Nice Restaurant ••

You can judge how precisely you must follow rules of etiquette by the fanciness of the restaurant. At a pizza place, just try not to drip cheese all over yourself, but at a nicer place, here are some things to keep in mind.

✔ In the U.S., when cutting food use the fork, turned over with tongs pointing down, in your left hand and the knife in your right hand. Once you've cut a bite-sized piece, you can put the knife down, transfer the fork to your right hand, and eat the piece you just cut. In Europe, leave the fork in your left hand. This is also acceptable in the U.S. and more efficient since you avoid all of the switching.

✔ When served soup, it is proper to scoop away from your body, to fill the spoon only partway, to sip (not slurp), and not to tilt the bowl at the end.

✔ When you're not using your dirty utensils, lay them flat together on your plate. Crossing them over your plate indicates to the server that you are still eating, and placing them parallel on the right side of the plate indicates that you want seconds.

✔ When you are finished with your meal, the proper way to signal the server that you're done is to place your utensils, with the handles pointing toward the right, either horizontally down the middle of the plate or with the tips pointing toward 11:00 and the knife blade facing you.

•• Choosing Wine ••

In a fancy restaurant, ask for the sommelier's wine recommendations. Subtly indicate your price range and whether you'd like red or white... this can be done by pointing to a particular bottle and asking about it. The sommelier, a professional, will note that you are looking for a $30 bottle, not an $80 one. If you're at a normal place, it's enough to know which wines are red and which are white. Reds tend to be a little heavier than whites, and most wine is either characterized as "dry" or "fruity."

Vocabulary they didn't teach you: When referring to wine, "fruity" means sweet and "dry" is the opposite. A "sommelier" is a wine steward, a waiter whose full-time job is to worry about wine.

Order by the glass so that you're not stuck with a whole bottle. Have a wine-tasting night with friends where you all order a different type of wine and try them all. Keep in mind that the same brands of wine taste different each year. So, even if you liked the 1998 Chianti you had last time, you may still want to order by the glass if the same brand is only available from the 2000 batch. Tasting will give you a general idea of what you like and will help you know what to order in the future. For now, just worry about red vs. white, and you won't look silly.

- ✓ **Popular Reds:** Chianti, Merlot, Cabernet Sauvignon, Gamays (used in Beaujolais, Zinfandel, Sirahs, and Pinot Noir).

- ✓ **Popular Whites:** Chardonnay, Pinot Grigio, Savignon Blanc, Pinot Blanc, Reisling, Gewürztraminer, Semillon, and Chenin Blanc. Basically anything with "blanc" in the name will be a white since "blanc" means white in French.

In the summer, also think about ordering vin roses, which are pink (in between red and white).

Conclusion

If you have read this book from cover to cover, then you should be pretty set to take care of any little glitches that come your way. There are a few things, however, that they didn't teach you in school and you do need to know that have not been specifically covered. Most of them can be summed up with the following thoughts: Pay attention to what is going on around you, and you will often be able to find solutions to problems before they get out of hand. Don't take yourself too seriously, and nothing will feel too serious to handle. Be generous with yourself and others, and you will always have friends to help you out of tight spots.

Stay calm, think things through, refer to this book as necessary, and when you learn new tricks of your own, write them down in the Notes section at the end of this book. Use your new skills wisely on all of your adventures in the real world and beyond. Congratulations and good luck!

Acknowledgments

I would like to thank the many people who helped me put this book together. Thanks first of all to everyone at Rabbit's Foot Press and to Josh for making this happen and for the wonderful introduction to publishing. I would also like to thank: Sam, who gave me the seed for this book and does the best chicken impression I have ever seen; everyone at West House, who shared their favorite tricks with me; everyone who e-mailed me about what they wished they knew or what they thought everyone else should know (and who provided some of the best quotes in the book); Mom, Dad, and Grandma, who have been teaching me all along, who are superb role models, and who gave me substantial reading and editing help; my little brother, Eric, who lent his "help" and jokes — I'll be sure to return the favor someday, buddy; my zoomie-roomie Emily, the crew at 73 Barnes, and my old pal Chris (who is now a "doctor"), who all deserve many thanks for editing, contributing, and keeping me in line; my teachers and friends, who were the best cheerleaders anyone could ask for; and last, but certainly not least, Brett, who is a much better speller than I am and who makes me laugh when I need it. He is thoughtful and patient and lovingly lets me get away with more than anyone else. He not only read and proofread this book more times than I did, but he also took me out into the driveway and taught me how to change a tire. This book is for Lily, my little sister and the light of my life (thanks, Mom).

About the Author

Emily Beatrice Caroline Falk, world traveler, cook, fix-it master, brain scientist, and big sister extraordinaire, graduated from Brown University with the class of '04. After graduation, Emily drove cross-country to live in Vancouver, BC, on a Fulbright Grant to study health policy (see Scholarships and Grants, page 81). She found a new apartment, bikes around the city for exercise, and eats well on a budget. She gets along with her new roommate and often talks to her mom on the phone while cooking (see Multitasking, page 73).

Notes

Notes

Notes

Notes